THE

FAMILY KITCHEN GARDENER;

CONTAINING

PLAIN AND ACCURATE DESCRIPTIONS

OF ALL THE

DIFFERENT SPECIES AND VARIETIES

OF

CULINARY VEGETABLES;

WITH

THEIR BOTANICAL, ENGLISH, FRENCH, AND GERMAN NAMES, ALPHABETICALLY ARRANGED, AND THE BEST MODE OF CULTIVATING THEM, IN THE GARDEN OR UNDER GLASS; WITH A DESCRIPTION OF IMPLEMENTS AND MEDICINAL HERBS IN GENERAL USE.

ALSO,

DESCRIPTIONS AND CHARACTERS OF THE MOST SELECT FRUITS, THEIR MANAGEMENT, PROPAGATION, ETC.

ILLUSTRATED WITH TWENTY-FIVE ENGRAVINGS.

BY ROBERT BUIST,

AUTHOR OF THE AMERICAN FLOWER-GARDEN DIRECTORY, ROSE MANUAL, ETC.

NEW YORK:

C. M. SAXTON, BARKER & CO., 25 PARK ROW.

SAN FRANCISCO: H. H. BANCROFT & CO.

1861.

CONTENTS.

TABLE DES MATIERES.

INHALT.

PREFACE.

Gardening is one of those occupations that combines pleasure with healthful employment. Reason and history unite in regarding it as the first pursuit that engaged the attention of man.

The fruits of the Garden are appreciated by all, and contribute much to the pleasures and comforts of life. But many possess gardens unworthy of the name: for want of a knowledge of their management they are unable, in season, to supply the wants of their own table. To remedy this deficiency is the object of this compendium. Into it nothing has been admitted that is not of the most practical character. It may be received as THE RESULT OF THIRTY YEARS' EXPERIENCE AND OBSERVATION ON THE CULTIVATION OF VEGETABLES AND FRUITS. To have given the reason for many of the operations recommended, or the process by which certain conclusions have been arrived at, would have enlarged the volume without adding to the value of the advice. It has been the object of the author to describe the preparation of the soil, the mode of culture, and the best varieties of every fruit or vegetable for market or family supply, in the plainest language, and most concise terms. The subjects are arranged in alphabetical order, so that any one, in an instant, for any part of the United States, may see *how to cultivate*, *when* and *what to sow*, and *when to reap*. Hitherto the works on this subject have been merely repetitions of European writers, not at all adapted to our climate; or when compiled with some degree of consideration as to that, yet simply the names of vegetables have been given, allowing the gardener or amateur, unguided, to select whatever might strike his fancy, without enabling him to supply his wants. In this Manual will be found a short but faithful description of the best vegetables and fruits; their period of maturity or their relative earliness or lateness, with their Botanical, English, French, and German names—a facility not met with in any similar work we have ever seen.

We have omitted a few vegetables of a coarse description, principally raised for cattle, by field culture. Among which are the *Portugal*, and *Cow Cabbage.* The former appeared lately as a new vegetable, under the name of *Coure Tronchuda*, though cultivated twenty years ago under the former name. The latter, also an old vegetable, created some excitement a few years ago; but the mania having died away, it finds its merited place.

The Fruits have been arranged in the order of their attaining maturity, and only the best in their season have been selected. It is presumed that the list will be found a certain guide to those who wish to grow only the best and most prolific sorts. Some selection of this kind has for some time been imperatively called for, by the wants of the gardener, farmer, and amateur, the multiplicity of sorts in the larger works and catalogues rendering them nearly useless to those who merely wish to know those kinds adapted for family or market supply. In illustrating our subject we have endeavored to avoid the use of all technical words, and to make every thing so plain that it can be comprehended by the most illiterate.

In conclusion, if this little manual be the means of diffusing a knowledge of vegetable culture more generally,—of adding to the pleasures of rural life,—of increasing the interest taken in horticultural pursuits; or guiding the gentleman, farmer, or student, in the occupation of his leisure hours, it will have attained the objec of

THE AUTHOR.

Philadelphia, Feb., 1847

BUIST'S

FAMILY KITCHEN GARDENER.

THE FORMATION OF A VEGETABLE OR KITCHEN GARDEN, &c.

Before proceeding with the subject of vegetable culture, the attention of the reader is requested to some remarks on the formation of a Kitchen Garden. This subject is forced upon us by a knowledge of how much labor and money are expended in producing one misplaced, badly designed, and unproductive—a most unpleasant attendant upon a country life; when, by the same labor and expense, one could have been obtained that would have yielded liberally every pleasure, every comfort, and even every luxury for a bountiful table.

The *situation* most suitable is a very gentle inclination toward the east or south-east, that it may have all the advantages of the morning sun. The next preferable exposure is south or south-west; if sheltered from the north or north-west, so much the better. However, avoid the neighborhood of large and spreading trees, as their roots will exhaust the soil, and their shade injure the crops.

In selecting *the ground*, it is of vast importance to have the soil of a healthy quality, being mellow, dry, and capable of being worked with the spade. The best soils are of a friable and loamy texture; the worst, those of a very light sandy or of a stiff clayey description.

If the bottom or subsoil be retentive, trench the ground at

least eighteen inches deep: good vegetables can never be produced on sour soil, nor on thin soil of only a few inches depth. Care and attention are necessary in *trenching*, as on the proper disposition at first the after good will follow. I most decidedly condemn the mode of trenching ground generally recommended; that is, to bury the top spit, and turn up the cold, sour subsoil. Experience has taught me another lesson: Open the first trench two feet wide, by putting aside the top spit *spade deep;* then turn up the bottom, where it lies, at least the full depth of the spade, in the same manner as in digging; throw the top of the next trench on the top of the first subsoil, and so on, till the whole is finished. The general method of trenching is to turn the top soil down and the subsoil up. This is attended with evil consequences, as many years will elapse before the bad soil, which has been turned up, can be made equal to the good soil, which has been turned down.

Another point we call attention to—*the inclination of the soil.* Some authors in this country merely publish the ideas of those of Europe, without regard to their applicability to this climate, and have recommended an inclination of one foot in from fifteen to twenty feet. Such a declivity would, during our heavy rains, sweep soil, manure, seeds, &c., to the lowest ground. An inclination of one foot in forty, or merely sufficient to carry off the water, is all that is requisite. However, the means have frequently to be adapted to the ends. If the situation be necessarily on the side of a rising ground, throw it at once into terraces of any required breadth. Let the steeps be covered with turf, to prevent the washing away of the soil, and arrange the planes into sub-divisions for culture.

The shape or figure of a Garden is a point of little consequence, though the square, or any form approaching it, is the best and most convenient. The boundary lines may be of any form, but the interior sub-divisions work to the best advantage in even lines. With regard to size, that, of course, must depend upon the number of the family, and may vary from a quarter to a whole acre. The walks may be from three to six feet wide, straight or serpentine—the former preferred, however. Where fancy may dictate, the latter can be adopted, cropping the curves of the ground with flowers, fancy plants, or choice fruits.

Rotation of Crops.—I admit that the same vegetable can be grown upon the same spot with success, year after year, but I also assert that a rotation of crops will be more productive, which is of great importance in culinary gardening; therefore never grow exhausting crops in succession. Substitute those alternately of as different roots and constitution as possible. Keep these objects in view, and even with ordinary management we vouch for a crop. Assiduity in the destruction of weeds, neatness and cleanliness, a constant stirring of the soil, digging deep and manuring freely, must be the constant companions of the gardener; making the business a source of pleasure, profit and advantage to himself, and an object of admiration to others.

Of Manures.—We may here premise that no garden will be worth its culture, unless well supplied with manure every year. The present day is a period of considerable agitation on this all-important subject. We have tried several of the new manures, some of them to our loss and (when we have departed from the stable yard) few to our advantage. In Europe great attention has been given to this subject, and many specifics recommended, which, when tried, have had frequently uncertain results, though in particular cases they have been crowned with success. In this country, however, our resources of domestic materials are abundant, and on every farm and garden much goes to waste. All weeds and useless vegetables, sweepings of walks, &c., should be dug into the ground at once. The dung of domestic birds, compounded with fresh soil, is a great renovator; but, if applied by itself, use it sparingly. *Guano* can only be safely applied in solution, one pound to five gallons of water—the liquid to be used when the vegetables are in a growing state. *Gypsum* is beneficial, but not of any duration. *Poudrette* is a very active manure, highly exciting to early crops. The safest and best of all manures are the combined deposits of the horse, the cow, and the pig; these, thrown into a heap to ferment, saturating it with all the soap-suds and urine that can be collected, will form the best, the safest, and most permanent manure, not equalled by any or all of the nostrums of the age. It may be applied at the rate of from twenty to thirty tons per acre. This quantity is not too much, when a garden is regularly cultivated. It requires no adept in vegetable culture to take at least two crops a year from the ground. Lime is not genial to the growth of vegetables; its principal function as a manure appears to be, to dissolve the organic matter in the soil and facilitate its decay. Soils of a sour, heavy nature, full of thready, undecomposed vegetable fibre, are greatly benefited by a dressing of air-slacked lime; but on rich soils, well cultivated, its effects are unfavorable to the growth of culinary vegetables.

ON IMPLEMENTS.

It is not our intention to go into a detail of all the useful articles connected with the culture of the garden, which would take us beyond our limits. Our object will be only to point out those most useful and essential to carry on the cultivation of the soil. The materials of which they are composed are chiefly of iron and wood; the best quality of both should be used, nothing purchased merely for its being *cheap*. The cheapest is the best and most durable to accomplish the end.

The spade is a very common tool, and should be of steel, with a hickory or ash handle, having two rivets through its head. No. 2, of the manufactory, is the most convenient size. Some American spades are equal to any of British manufacture.

The *Rake* (Fig. 1) should be of the best wrought iron, with teeth about $2\frac{1}{2}$ inches long and $1\frac{1}{2}$ apart. The head is of any size, from six to twenty inches. There are also rakes of malleable iron, and wooden rakes with steel teeth: the latter sort are very convenient for rough ground. The handle should be round, made of pine, or any other light wood, and from six to eight feet long.

Fig. 1.

Beet Rake (Fig. 2).—This very useful implement is composed of hard wood, with steel teeth, obtusely pointed, about two inches wide, five inches long, and from nine to twelve inches apart. It is exceedingly useful for drawing drills in which to sow Beets, Carrots, Onions, and all small seeds or roots. In using it, strain the line, and draw with some strength; when three drills will be made at once, saving the labor of moving the line so frequently as when the work is accomplished by the hoe.

Fig. 2.

Hoes are of many and varied descriptions, sizes and shapes. Fig. 3 gives an idea of the most useful. They should be of the very best of steel, with rather strong, round handles, five feet long. They are in sizes from three to ten inches. Those of three, five, seven and nine inches are generally used.

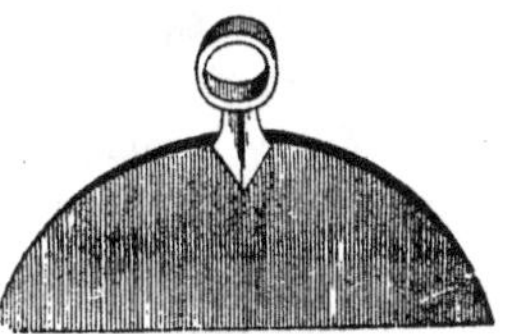
Fig. 3.

Pronged Hoes, Fig. 4, are very useful, indeed indispensable, for stirring the soil and destroying weeds. They are of steel or malleable iron; the latter generally used, though the former is preferable; handles four and a half feet long

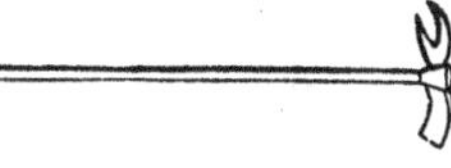
Fig. 4.

The *Dutch, or Scuffle Hoe*, Fig. 5, is very useful for cleaning walks and cutting weeds where the ground is of a light nature. It is also called a Thrust Hoe (being used by pushing from you) in contradistinction to the Draw Hoe, Fig. 3., which is best adapted for all heavy work.

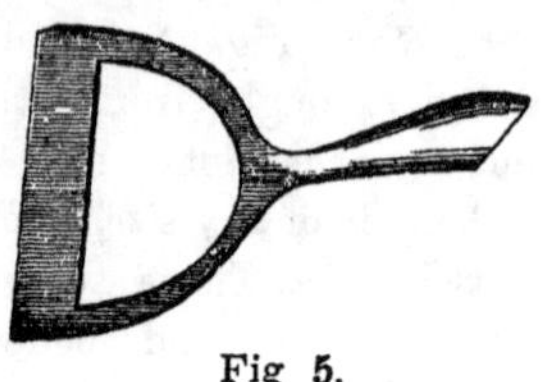

Fig 5.

The Reel and Line, Fig 6. The reel is of wood or iron; the latter is preferable. It consists of two parts, the shank and the head. The head turns round on the shank and winds up the line or cord, which can be of any length.

Fig. 6.

The Trowel, Fig. 7, is very useful for removing plants and lifting them with balls of earth for transplanting. It should be of the best iron or steel, with a square socket into the handle, and from five to nine inches long, exclusive of the handle.

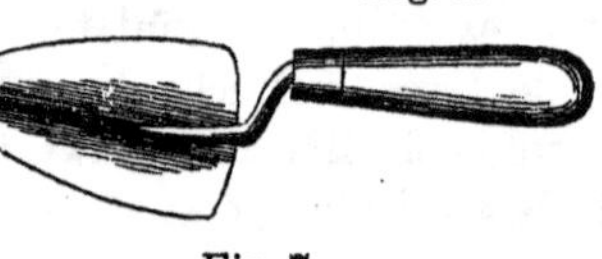

Fig. 7.

The *Dibber* is a short piece of round wood, generally made from an old spade or shovel handle, about one and a half feet long, obtusely pointed, frequently shod with iron on the one end, and conveniently formed for the hand on the other. It should be well made, as it is of very general use, and if iron-shod, will last half a century.

Garden Watering-pot.—Of this utensil there are several sizes; those that hold from three to four gallons are of the proper dimensions; they should be made of the best double tin, having two roses—the one pierced with holes the twentieth, the other the fortieth part of an inch. Keep them well painted, and when not in use, the mouth downwards.

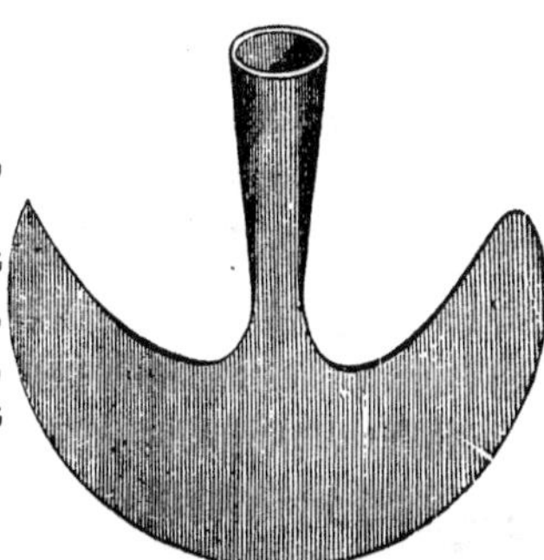

The Grass-edging Iron or Knife, Fig. 8, is for cutting the turf of grass borders or walks. It should be of the very best steel, with a round, strong handle, about three and a half feet long.

Fig. 8.

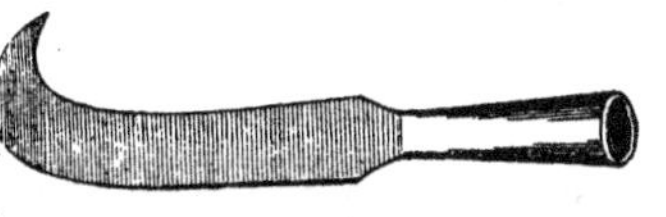

Garden Hook, Fig. 9, for dressing hedges, made of the very best steel, having a handle of an oval form, of strong wood, 3½ feet long, and of a small size, that the hand may conveniently grasp it

Fig 9.

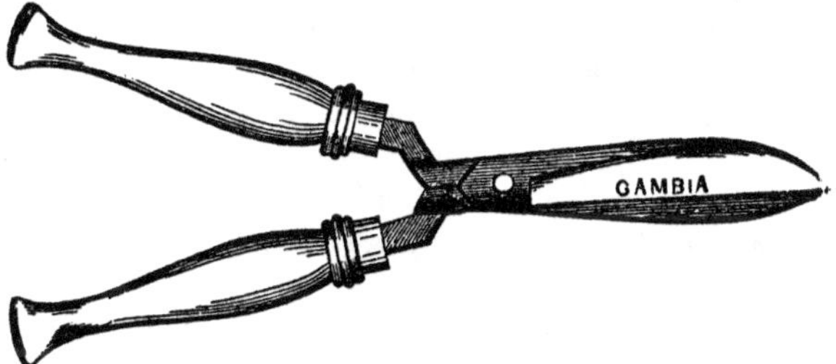

Fig. 10.

Garden Shears, Fig. 10, are of various sizes, from six to twelve inch blades, and used for cutting edgings of Box, clipping hedges, and many other purposes. They are of great variety and quality. The seven and nine-inch sizes are most convenient.

Ladies' Shears, Fig. 11. These are of the very best material, neatly made, for the use of ladies who take a delight in gardening operations.

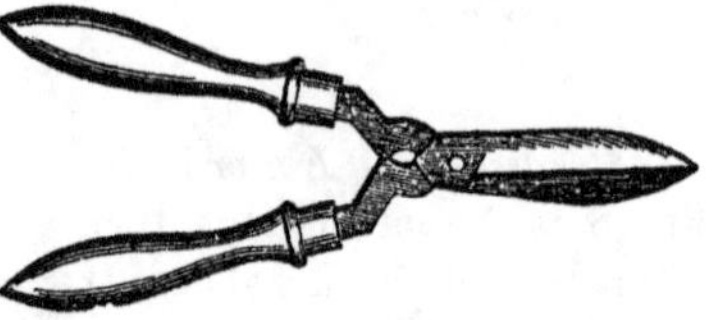

Fig. 11.

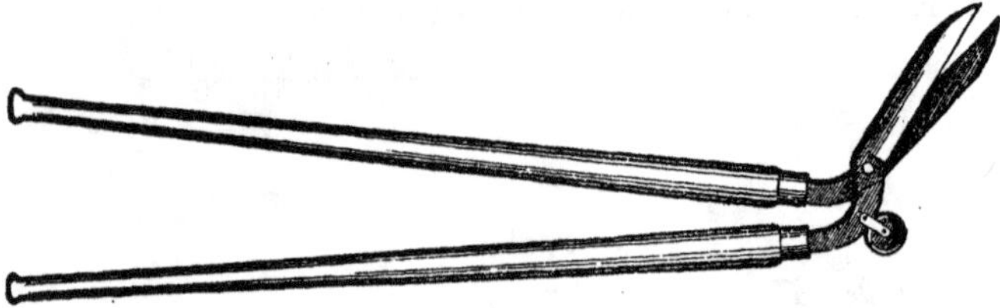

Fig. 12.

Grass-edging Shears, Fig. 12. These are made expressly for cutting grass-edgings, and have a wheel that rests on the walk while the shears trim off the grass. It is a very convenient and expeditious implement.

Hand-Glass, Fig. 13. These are made of red cedar, or cast iron. The latter is most neat and durable. It consists of two parts, the bottom and top. A useful utensil for growing seeds of early Celery, Tomato, Egg-plant, or any other article of early culture; also well adapted for covering Cauliflower plants where the winters are not very severe. When air is to be given to the plants enclosed, it is done by lifting up the top and replacing it diagonally; by this means air is freely admitted. A glass case may be made of any height with these hand-glasses, by merely placing the bottom frames one upon the other. Those we use are of cast iron, and cost $3.50 each.

Fig. 13.

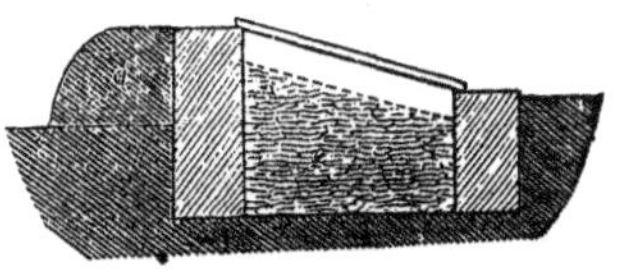
Fig. 14.

A Sunk Pit, Fig. 14, is in part in the earth and partly above it, by forming sides of brick, stone, locust, chestnut, or cedar boards. On these, glass frames are sometimes placed, and at other times only mats or shutters. Such pits answer for the preservation of vegetables, such as Endive, Celery, Lettuce, Cauliflower, Broccoli, &c. Air is given on all occasions when it can be done with safety, by propping up the sash or shutters.

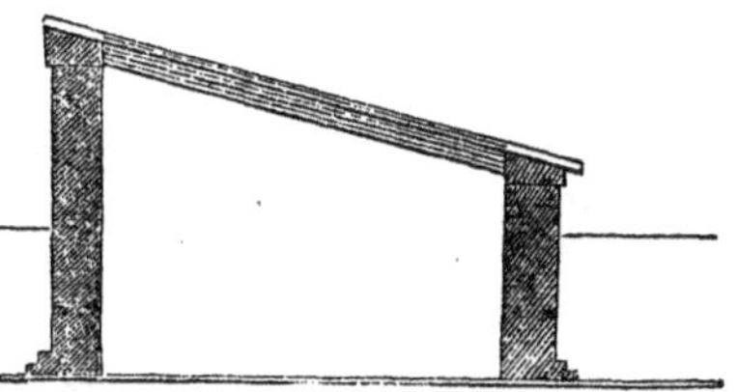
Fig. 15.

The Walled Pit, Fig. 15, is also partly sunk in the ground and partly out. The walls are formed of brick or stone, finished with a wooden or stone coping, the width of the wall, into which cross rafters are mortised (but moveable) to support the sashes. Our object in having them moveable is to admit of their being raised as the growth of Cauliflowers or any other plants require. This is readily done by having a strong two-inch plank made to fit the back and front of the pit, and to rest on the coping; the rafters to rest on these planks either by mortising holes for their reception, or to have them to rest on clets. This is a great convenience, and overcomes the difficulty every grower feels when his Cauliflowers touch the glass.

There is no appendage to the garden of greater utility than this pit. It is two feet under ground, one foot above it in front, and two feet above it at the back, and six or seven feet wide in the clear. It is an excellent winter apartment for plants when covered with sash and mats. When filled with very rich earth it grows fine Cauliflowers, that will be in use from March to

May. If filled with warm manure early in February, it will grow Cucumbers that will be in use from April to July, or grow Radishes and small sallading in quantity. In summer the sashes can be used for growing fine varieties of Grapes. See our article on *Fruits*.

Sash Light, Fig. 16. Made of yellow or the best seasoned white pine, 1½ to 2 inches thick. The sash should be 3 feet 8 inches wide, and 6 or more feet long; the glass we prefer is 6 by 6, or 6 by 8, and of the best quality. The wood must have two coats of oil paint before glazing, and at least one coat afterwards. All the glass must be bedded in soft putty; the laps of the glass should not exceed half an inch: one-fourth of an inch, if well done, is quite sufficient. A sash well painted and protected when not in use, will last from thirty to forty years. The smaller the panes of glass the less will be the damage from breakage.

Fig. 16.

The Common Hot-Bed Frame is a box of wood, bottomless, of any length or breadth to suit the object in view, but generally six feet wide and from six to sixteen feet long, highest at the side to be placed to the north, and subdivided by cross-bars, and each division covered by a glazed sash. The component parts of the above frame, instead of being mortised into one another, should be fastened with hooks and staples, or keyed iron bolts, which easily admit of their being taken asunder and put under cover when they are not wanted for use. I have about a hundred sashes that can be taken apart and stowed away, or erected in one day.

Vegetable or Kitchen Garden, with a select assortment of Fruit combined, Fig. 17. This arrangement affords great facilities for croping the ground and a rotation of crops. It also confines the trees to one place, for the purpose of giving a partial shade to the main walk in summer, without injuring any of the vegetables. This plan is decidedly preferable to the mode of distributing the trees over the garden.

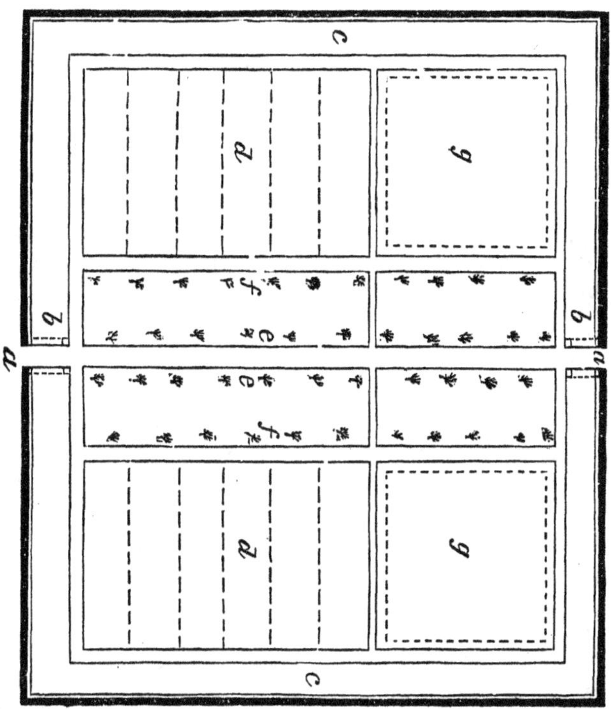

Fig. 17.

a a—Main entrance.

b b—Grape-vine arbor.

c c—A border ten or twelve feet wide all round the garden, for the smaller and finer sorts of vegetables.

d d—Compartments for vegetables in quantity, divided by alleys.

e e—Row of choice Pear trees on each side of the walk, affording shade.

f f—Rows of dwarf trees, either Plum, Quince, Peach on the Plum stock, Apricots, or dwarf Pears.

g g—Large compartments, surrounded by Currant and Raspberry bushes, for early Corn, early Potatoes, or any vegetable of which a large quantity is grown. If situation will admit of it, the pits or frames can be in these quarters portioned off by a low hedge.

GARDEN SEEDS FOR HALF AN ACRE.

The following seeds, with judicious management, will fully crop a garden of half an acre, which will supply a moderate sized family with vegetables throughout the year. Vegetable seeds, where carefully grown in this country, are (with a few exceptions) preferable to those imported; but the utter carelessness manifested by many in keeping them apart when growing, is not to be recommended.

1 oz. Asparagus.	4 oz. Mustard.
3 qts. Beans, of sorts.	½ oz. Melons.
4 oz. Beet, of sorts.	½ oz. Okra.
¼ oz. Broccoli.	2 oz. Onions, sorts.
¼ oz. Cauliflower.	1 pap. Parsley.
4 oz. Cabbage, of sorts.	1 oz. Parsneps.
¼ oz. Celery.	1 pap. Peppers.
8 oz. Cress.	½ oz. Pumpkin.
½ oz. Cucumber.	8 qts. Peas.
1 oz. Carrot.	8 oz. Radish.
1 qt. Early Corn.	½ oz. Salsafy.
1 pkt. Egg Plant.	½ oz. Squash.
½ oz. Endive.	8 oz. Spinage.
¼ oz. Leek.	1 pap. Tomatoes.
1 qt. Lima Beans.	2 oz. Turnip.
1 oz. Lettuce, of sorts.	6 pap. Pot and Sweet Herbs.

Cost about $10.

Seeds should always be kept in bags, in a dry, airy situation. Wall closets and cellars are objectionable, from their dampness. All seeds will keep two, and many from three to six years.

ARTICHOKE.

Cy'nara Scólymus—Artichaut, Fr.—*Artischoke*, Ger.

THE Artichoke is principally cultivated in the gardens of the French, by whom it is considered more as a luxury than a profitable esculent. There are two varieties, the *Globe* and the *Green;* the former is so called from its globular head, of a dull, purplish tint. The scales are turned in at the top more than the other variety, and it is preferred, as the scales, or edible parts, are thicker and possess most flavor. The *Green* is more hardy and prolific, the scales are more open, and the plant better adapted for culture in cold climates than the former.

The heads in their immature state, and before their blue, thistle-like flowers open, are cut and boiled in salt and water; the edible part is merely the fleshy substance on the bottom of the scales, which, to make palatable, has to be dipped in a nicely prepared sauce of butter and spices. They are frequently, however, eaten as a salad in a raw state.

CULTURE.—It is propagated from seeds, or by division of the young suckers that arise from the roots of the old plants in Spring. They are fit to slip or cut off after they have made a few roots and leaves. Plant them three feet apart each way, in soil well-prepared by digging and manuring; water each plant freely, and occasionally if the weather continues dry, till they have taken root; keep constantly stirring the soil, and destroying the weeds. On the approach of winter remove all decayed leaves—although it appears a very strong plant, yet north of Virginia it requires more or less protection, and may be covered with the earth taken from between the rows, and drawn well up round the roots. In very severe seasons, an additional covering of dry litter or branches is advisable. In Spring remove all the litter, level down the soil, and examine the stools. Let those of the strongest grow to produce heads, the rest are removed by a pressure of the thumb or a cut with the knife. Dig the whole ground level, using yearly plenty of good rotten manure. A bed will continue productive for seven or more years. If the heads are not wanted for use or seed, they should be destroyed from the stem, which promotes the strength and vitality of the plant. Seed sown early in Spring, in drills, eighteen inches apart and two inches deep, will produce good plants the first season, and even be more permanent than those procured from offsets. Protect them carefully the first winter; transplant early in Spring, as above directed, for offsets. They will produce a few heads the following year, and thereafter a regular crop. If quality is preferred to quantity, the head that surmounts the stem only should be allowed to grow; all the lateral ones growing on the same stalk should be removed in their young state.

ASPARAGUS.

Aspáragus officinális—*Asperge*, Fr.—*Spargel*, Ger.

This universal vegetable is supposed to be a native of Great Britain, where it is found on banks of sandy soil contiguous to the sea, growing luxuriantly under the salt breezes. Cultivators have found that salt brine, or a thin covering of salt thrown over the beds in the Fall, before they have their final dressing, proves very beneficial to its growth. Although it is not considered a very nutricious vegetable, yet it occupies a considerable proportion of every garden, and is extensively cultivated for our markets—some growers having eight or ten acres under culture, and I have no doubt that in a very few years it will be increased ten-fold.

Propagation.—This is accomplished only by seeds. When a new bed is formed, in order to save time, two or three-year old plants may be procured from Nurserymen or Gardeners, at a very low rate. There are several varieties of Asparagus named in catalogues, but there is a great similarity among them, and we will class them into two only, the *Green-top* and the *Purple-top*. The former is round in the top and of a bright green color. The latter of a purple reddish-green color, very close headed, and is the sort generally cultivated. There is another supposed variety called the *Giant*, which is greatly extolled by Seedsmen on account of its size, but I believe the principal secret lies in the quality of the soil and the superiority of culture. Sow the seed early in Spring, (about a pound will be sufficient for a family), thinly, in drills, one and a-half to two inches deep, and eighteen inches from row to row—in good, rich, sandy, loamy soil, well manured and prepared. Strong one-year old plants are much better for transplanting than those of even three years' old, when the growth has been indifferent. Rake the ground even, and keep it free from weeds by frequent hoeing. About the first of the following November, some stable litter should be spread over the ground, to keep the young roots from frost.

Culture.—The best ground for Asparagus is a light, sandy loam, at least two feet deep. Before planting it should be dug very deep or trenched in the way we have recommended, burying in plenty of manure, as no more can be supplied after the beds are planted (unless by surface dressings). The ground can scarcely be too rich, for the sweetness and tenderness of the shoots depend on the rapidity of the growth, which is greatly promoted by the richness of the soil. A plot of ground twenty feet wide and from forty to fifty feet long will be suitable for a moderate-sized family. Over it sow from fifty to one hundred pounds of salt, incorporating it with the soil to the depth of four or five inches. The ground having been well prepared and properly leveled, divide it off into beds four feet wide. with alleys of two feet between them. The work should all be done in fine weather, about the end of March. Drive in a strong stake at each corner, take up the plants carefully from the seed-rows with a fork, and expose them to the air as little as possible, keeping them covered during the time of planting, and not allowing the roots to get dry. Stretch a line lengthwise along the bed, nine inches from the edge, and with a spade cut a small furrow, six inches deep. Having the plants ready, set a row along the trench, nine inches apart, with the crown of the roots two inches below the surface, drawing a little earth upon them to fix them as placed. Having finished a row, cover them directly with the earth that has been thrown out of the furrow, raking it regularly and to an equal depth over the crown of the plants. Proceed to open another furrow a foot from the first; plant and finish it as above, when you will have four rows to each bed. After all is planted, rake the beds lengthwise, drawing off all stones and rubbish; dress the surface neatly and evenly. Let the edges be lined out in exact order, allowing two feet to each alley. As these alleys will be of little service the first season, and no waste ground should ever be seen in a garden, dig them up and plant a row of cabbage in each. Nothing further will be required during the Summer than to destroy all weeds. The following Winter cover them to the depth of three or four inches with rotten manure, to keep the crowns from sun and frost; if, in the Spring, the earth is found to have settled in any part, the deficiency must be made up with more mould. It is a common practice to sow Radishes upon the beds, but it is an injurious one, as it robs the ground of a great portion of its nutriment, so essential to their luxuriant growth. The plants are permitted the two first years to run up to stalks, that strong crowns may be formed at their base for the future crop.

After the third year, the beds will require the following mode of treatment. From the middle of October to the end of November give them their winter dressing, which consists in cutting down the stalks close to the ground and clearing the beds from weeds; drawing them off at the same time with a rake into the alleys, to be buried or taken to the compost heap to be mixed up with other litter and again returned to the soil. Cover the whole of the bed with two or three inches of ma nure; the alleys must be dug spade deep, at the same time spreading some soil over the manure on the beds, and leveling the whole evenly. It may be supposed that the annual dressing in this way will in a few years considerably raise the beds; but by the Spring forking and raking, together with the hoeing and dressing during Summer, a considerable portion of the earth is being continually drawn again into the alleys.

As soon as the frost is fairly out of the ground in the Spring, loosen the surface of the beds with a fork, introducing it three or four inches into the soil, turning up the earth with care not to wound the crown of the roots. Then make the surface of the beds even and equal, drawing off the rough earth, stones, &c., into the alleys; finish by stretching a line along the edge of the beds, and trim them neatly off with the spade. Stirring the bed in this manner enables the shoots to rise in free growth; admits the air, rain, and sunshine into the ground, and encourages the roots to produce buds of a strong size. A full crop may be expected the fourth season after planting. The proper method of cutting them is to scrape a little of the earth away from each shoot; then, with a sharp-pointed, long-bladed knife, cut off the shoot slantingly, about three inches under the surface, taking care not to wound the younger buds that are advancing below in different stages of growth. It is in the best state for cutting when it is four inches above ground, and while the top remains close and round. The cutting should never extend beyond the middle of June.

Asparagus beds, with good culture, will continue to give bountiful crops for twelve or fifteen years. It is frequently forced on dung hot-beds, and in the hands of the initiated, with great success; but to go into the general minutiæ of forcing vegetables, would take us entirely beyond our limits; a few hints however, will give an idea of the operation. Prepare a hot-bed of two lights, in the way we have directed for cucumbers, about two feet high at back and twenty inches in front. Cover it with four inches of soil; lay thereon roots that are at least four years old; cover them three inches with the same soil, and give the whole a copious watering. Admit air at the back by tilting the sash daily, in sunshine. In two weeks, or three at most, you may expect to be able to cut for the table. A bed of this sort will produce daily, or at least every two days, a dish for the table, and continue in bearing three or four weeks. The process may be carried to the extent of the demand. Where properly managed, it will fully compensate either as a luxury or a marketable article.

BASIL.

O'cymum Basílicum.—*Basilic*, Fr.—*Basilikum*, Ger.

There are two sorts of Basil, the sweet or large leaved, *Ocymum Basilicum;* and the small leaved or bush Basil, *Ocymum minimum.* The qualities of both are the same, but the former is principally used for culinary purposes. They are both annuals; the leaves or tops are the parts gathered for use. The French are very partial to the flavor of this plant; its leaves enter into the composition of many of their soups and sauces; and, on account of their strong flavor of cloves, are used in all highly-seasoned dishes, and even introduced into salads.

Culture.—The seeds should be sown on rich, light ground, about the middle of April, or it may be grown in a gentle hotbed with early salad, and transplanted to the open ground about the end of the month, in rows one foot apart and six inches from plant to plant. It makes a very good edging for some of the vegetable quarters. It is a tender plant and very easily injured by the early frosts of autumn, previous to which they should be pulled up by the roots, tied in small bunches, and hung up in an airy room or loft to dry. They will retain a great portion of their aromatic qualities for Winter use.

BEANS.

Phaseolus vulgàris.—*Haricot*, Fr.—*Schminkbohne*, Ger.

THIS vegetable is one of the standards of the garden for summer culture. It is an every-day dish for the table. The numerous forms in which it can be served up ; the rich, buttery flavor of some of the varieties; the crisp, juicy character of others, renders at least some of the family palatable to the most fastidious.

The following are *Bush-Beans*, or *Snap-Shorts*, and their characteristic of excellence is their breaking crisply. If tough, they are unfit for cooking. They are arranged in the rotation of their coming to maturity. Some growers prefer one variety only, while others prefer several sorts. Our remarks are all made with the articles under our culture, and notes taken on the spot. We pay no regard to the hacknied quotations handed down from one writer to another.

Early Mohawk.—A variety that resists more frost, as an early crop, than any other. It is an excellent bearer, pods long ; beans, when ripe, large, oval, dark speckled. Sown 13th May, fit for the table June 16th.

Early Six-Weeks.—Not so hardy as the former, but equally early. It is a light-colored Bean.

Early Valentine. — The Valentine Beans are extensively cultivated in this vicinity for the market. They are the sorts that have round pods, and continue on the plant a long period for culinary purposes. A great bearer, of a salmon color, with pink spots. Sown 13th May, fit for the table June 20th.

Yellow Six-Weeks.—In growth and maturity very similar to the former, though three days later.

Late Valentine, or Refugee.—A very excellent variety, very similar in appearance to the Early Valentine when green.

though a stronger grower. Color dark-brown, speckled. Sown 13th May, fit for use June 25th.

Black Valentine is a most excellent variety, a great bearer and of delicate flavor. Ripens a few days later than the former.

Royal White-Kidney.—The best late variety; has long pods, richly flavored, and for family use is indispensable, not only in its green state, but for Winter use. As a vegetable it is preferable to any other. Sown 13th May, fit for the table July 1st.

The above sorts may be sown at any time from the 10th of April to the 25th of August. The first sowing in Spring is frequently cut off with frost, though we have seen the Valentine sorts all killed, while the Mohawk stood uninjured. It should therefore always be adopted for the earliest sowing. A few rows of each sort sown every two weeks will keep a succession for the table from the first of June till the middle of October. As this crop does not long occupy the ground, it can frequently be sown between rows of Corn, ridges of Celery, or Drumhead Cabbage when they are first planted.

Culture.—Any good, light, rich soil will grow this Bean in perfection. Draw drills with the hoe two and a half inches deep, and from one foot to eighteen inches from row to row; drop the beans regularly therein, about two inches apart; cover up carefully and expeditiously; give frequent and deep hoeings to keep open the soil. As soon as the crop is three inches high, draw the earth to their stems. When they begin to show their flower bud, draw a few inches more, which is termed by gardeners, *earthing up.*

Seed.—Where seed is wished to be saved, the sorts must be grown apart, as far as practicable, for they are very susceptible of mixture, if even within fifty yards of each other.

Running or Pole Beans (*Haricot à rames*, Fr.; *Stangen bohue*, Ger.) are sorts in great esteem; especially the Lima, of which there are two varieties, the White and Green. Both are excellent in flavor. The latter has the advantage of size, and the former of producing a more certain and uniform [illegible] It is the variety most extensively cultivated for the Philadelphia market, covering an extent of over two hundred acres in the immediate vicinity of the city.

Culture.—They are planted in the last week of April, or first week of May, in hills very similar to Indian Corn, and about the same distance apart. In fact, those who can plant Corn, can plant Lima Beans; though strangers to this luscious vegetable often make very curious mistakes in its culture, some drawing drills and sowing them therein, others digging pits and burying the delicate seed (which is impatient of cold or moisture) six or eight inches deep; the results from both of which operations must be nearly a total failure. Some sprout these beans in a hot-bed, and transplant them into the hills in which they are to grow; but very little, if any time, is gained by the trouble. A hill of good, rich earth, raised a few inches above the level, and five or six beans put two inches deep therein, will be found the safest and surest. If three grow, it is enough; if not, plant over again. They will grow twenty feet; but rods of twelve feet, placed two feet in the ground at the time the hill is made, will support them. Cold damp weather frequently destroys the first and even the second planting.

Carolina or Sewee Bean, has all the habits of the Lima, though not so large. It is more hardy, and produces as profusely, but has not so much of the rich, buttery flavor.

Dutch-Case Knife is an excellent pole Bean, producing a good crop, of fine flavor, and much earlier for the table than either the Lima or Carolina. It can be used either in or with out the pod; it is also well adapted for Winter use.

Cranberry, both the *Red* and *White* are much cultivated though we decidedly prefer the latter. They are of the easiest culture; the corn-field can be used, if the garden does not suffice. In fact, we see no reason why every farmer should not have a few Beans, even of the *Lima*, on every corn-hill. The stalks would support the vines; the produce would bring four dollars per bushel; or even for family use, they would be profitable for an every-day vegetable the whole Winter; they are a certain crop, even preferable to the Potato, more nutritive, while the latter is becoming a precarious crop, and of an indifferent quality.

Scarlet Runners require to be earlier planted than the Lima Bean, that they may be well advanced in growth before the hot weather begins, which stunts their growth and prevents their blooming. They must be poled in the same way. The blossoms are red, hence their name.

Vicia Faba—Fève de Marais of the French, or Windsor Bean of the English—are of trifling value for this climate, compared with the sorts previously described. However, in cool climates, on rich loamy soil, they will, if planted early, make a return for the use of the ground, and prove a variety for the table. The Windsor and early Long Pod are the best varieties. Plant them in drills eighteen inches asunder, and two inches apart in the row.

BEET.

Bèta vulgàris.—Beterave, Fr.—*Rothe Rübe*, Ger.

The Beet is a native of the sea-coast of the south of Europe. It takes its name from the shape of its seed-vessel, which, when it swells with the seed, has the form of the letter beta (β) of the Greek alphabet.

There are several varieties of the Beet in cultivation for culinary purposes, but the most essential sorts are confined to the Long Blood and Turnip Rooted.

The Turnip Rooted is the earliest variety, and takes its name from the form of the root. Its quality is decided by the richness of color and closeness of the grain.

Long Blood is the sort run upon for a general crop, to use during Winter and Spring It often grows twelve or fourteen inches long and four or five inches thick. Beet is used and prepared for the table in a great variety of ways. It is boiled and sliced, and eaten cold with vinegar; it is sliced in salads, both as an eatable and a garnish; it also makes a beautiful and agreeable pickle. The root itself, if eaten alone, affords but little nourishment, though quite indispensable on a table of any pretensions.

White Beet is esteemed only for its stalks, or the mid-rib of the leaves, which, being divested of the leafy part, improves the flavor of soups; or if peeled and stewed, it can be eaten like Asparagus.

Radish-rooted Beet is a new variety, of a very dark blood-red color; in shape very similar to the long scarlet Radish, though much larger.

Whyte's New Blood-Beet is an improvement in richness of color on the old Long Beet.

London Blood-Beet is a new variety, with something more than a name. We are as particular at our table in discussing the qualities of vegetables as others are in the cut or the joint, or the peculiar flavors of Port or Madeira, and we feel assured that this variety of the Beet is more delicate in flavor, more brilliant in color, and of as good a form as any other sort.

Silver or Sea-Kale Beet very much resembles the White Beet, though the ribs of the leaves are larger, and, when cooked, has much of the flavor of sea-kale. There are several other sorts which come more under the notice of the agriculturist, such as Sugar Beet, Mangel-Wurtzel, &c.

CULTURE.—Little art is requisite for the culture of this vegetable. One grand essential for an early crop is to dig deep and manure well Sow as soon as the soil will admit of work ing, after the frost is out of the ground; draw drills half an inch deep and eighteen inches apart; drop the seeds therein about three inches apart, cover them lightly and rake finely; if the ground be dry, tread or roll them firmly. Sow a light sprinkling of early Radish seed before raking. They will be fit for pulling before the Beets are ready for thinning, which will be in four or five weeks. As soon as the Beets have made a few leaves, thin them out to six inches apart, allowing the strongest plants to remain. For a full Winter crop, sow the Long Blood or London Beet at any time from the 20th of May till the 20th of June. These will keep better and be more tender for Winter use than those sown earlier. On the approach of frost, about the end of October, take up the roots; cut the leaves off within two inches of the crown, and put the roots away in a dry cellar, or pack them in barrels with dry sand, and keep from severe frost. Plant out early in Spring a few of the best roots for seed; avoid those of a rough or fibrous nature.

BORECOLE.

Bràssica oleràcea, var.—*Chou vert*, Fr.—*Grüne Kohl*, Ger.

Borecole, German Greens, or Scotch Kale, is a very delicate vegetable. It is essential to its perfection that it be fully acted upon by frost before it is cut for the kitchen. There are several varieties of it. The parts used are the top or crown of the plant, with any of the side sprouts. It boils well, and is tender and sweet. The tall and dwarf curly sorts are best adapted for garden culture. Sow the seed in April, along with other Cabbage, which transplant and treat in the same manner

BROCCOLI.

Brássica oleràcea, var.—*Broccoli*, Fr.—*Italianische Kohl*, Ger.

Broccoli is a variety of the Cabbage closely related to the Cauliflower, though not so delicate in flavor as that vegetable. It is supposed to have come originally from the island of Cypress, and was cultivated nearly two hundred years ago. In mild climates it is extensively used from November to March, the various early and late sorts coming to maturity in the very middle of Winter. In this latitude the culture is confined to Grange's *Early White* and the *Early Purple Cape*. In their growth, habit, and eatable parts, they resemble Cauliflower, all of them forming roundish heads in the centre of their leaves, composed entirely of a compact collection of numerous buds or tender advancing shoots.

Grange's Early produces large, fine, white, compact heads, of a conical shape. The leaves cover the heads and afford protection in frosty weather. This sort is so much like Cauliflower that those who ought to be judges have pronounced it such, though the leaves and flavor are entirely different. For a good crop, sow the seed early in April.

Early Purple Cape also produces large sized heads, of a reddish brown color; when genuine, very close and compact. It is rather earlier than the former, and more hardy.

The Dwarf Tartarian, White Malta, and Late White are fine sorts for a mild climate. They will be in use the whole Winter. Sow the seeds in June, and transplant in July, in very rich sandy loam.

Culture.—The seeds should be sown in April and May, in rich soil, on an open exposure, where the plants grow much stronger than near trees or fences. Sow the seeds tolerably thick on the surface; if dry, tramp them down and rake in lightly, if drought continues, give the beds a few waterings till the plants appear, which will be in two weeks. Transplant in June or July, when the weather is moist, in rows two feet apart and twenty inches in the row. If the weather is dry when planted, give them water every other day till they begin to grow. Their further culture is to keep them clear of weeds by hoeing and stiring the ground; when they have advanced in growth, draw some earth to their stems, which greatly promotes their luxuriance.

They commence heading in October and continue till destroyed by severe frost. The heads should be cut while they remain close, and before they assume a seedy-like appearance.

In this, and more northern latitudes, it is necessary to put these plants into a shed or cellar, to have them during Winter. Lift them carefully before severe frost, and plant them in earth. They will head well when thus treated, but south of Virginia this vegetable may be had in perfection without the least trouble, excepting the culture. The seed is all imported from Europe.

BRUSSELS SPROUTS.

Brássica oleràcea, var.—*Chou de Bruxelles*, Fr.—*Sprossen. Kohl*, Ger.

This variety of the Cabbage is supposed to have originated from the Savoy. It is a celebrated vegetable in Europe, especially near Bruxelles and other large towns in Flanders, where, from October to April, it is an every-day dish on the table of both the rich and the poor. Till recently very little attention has been given to it in this country.

Culture.—Sow the seed in April, and transplant in June, or July, in the same manner as Broccoli. The leaves of the plant are similar to the Savoy, crowning a stem about two feet high, from which grow out numerous little cabbages of from one to two inches in diameter. After the sprouts have been frosted (which is necessary to their perfection) they may be gathered. Immerse them in clear water for an hour, and cleanse them from dust and insects; then boil them quickly for about twenty minutes, using plenty of water. When soft, take them up and drain them well. They are then to be put into a stew-pan with cream, or with a little butter thickened with flour, and seasoned to taste, stirring them thoroughly. They may be served up to table with tomato sauce, which greatly heightens their flavor: or seasoned with pepper and salt, and eaten with any sort of meat. As this vegetable is comparatively little known, I have made these observations with a view of encouraging its culture. Plants for seed should have their tops cut off, and the little cabbages allowed to shoot, from which the seed is more perfect. It will keep fresh and sound in a dry place three years, but when grown for that object should not be near any other sort of Cabbage.

BURNET.

Potèrium Sanguisórba—Petite Pimprenelle, Fr.—*Pimpernelle*, Ger.

Burnet is a hardy perennial plant. The parts made use of are the young leaves, which are put into salads, and by the French very frequently into soups, to which it gives a pleasant and warm taste.

Culture.—Seed may be sown early in Spring, in a row, where they are to remain. Twenty plants will be sufficient for any family. They are also propagated by dividing the roots, and as the young luxuriant leaves are preferable, the plants should be manured every year, and renewed every three or four years.

2*

CABBAGE.

Brássica oleràcea, var.—*Chou pomme*, Fr.—*Weiss Kopf-kohl*, Ger.

The Cabbage is one of the most ancient and esteemed vegetables, and as an esculent it stands in the highest estimation. The name is applied to the firm head or ball that is formed by the leaves folding close over each other. Like all other cultivated plants, the Cabbage has undergone so many changes and assumed so many varieties that it is not easy to give a description that will apply to the whole. Without exaggeration, many of the sorts are as far superior to others in flavor as cream is to sour milk, yet we continue to grow, year after year, the same varieties; some of which are so rank and strong that they are only fit for the cattle-yard or cow-shed, to the neglect of others which are not only tender and delicious to the taste, but are truly agreeable to the olfactory organs. The principal varieties in cultivation are the following.

Early York.—This is a valuable early variety, which has been cultivated upwards of one hundred years. Its earliness, and delicate taste and flavor, keeps it in estimation. The heads are small, round, slightly heart-shaped, and very firm. From its very dwarf growth, a great many can be planted in a small space. Rows one foot apart, and eight inches from plant to plant.

Large York. A variety of the former, of larger growth, and fully two weeks later. It is the variety cultivated extensively for the markets about Philadelphia.

Late York is another variety, improved in size, but inferior in flavor, and is, under the same culture, three weeks later than the Early York.

Early Nonpareil is one of the best sorts in cultivation. It heads freely, and is of a good size, and very delicate flavor.

Early Vanack is another sweet and delicately flavored variety; in shape very similar to the Early York, though larger, and a little later. The flavor is equal, if not superior to that universally esteemed sort.

Early Battersea is a roundish, oval-headed variety. It is most excellent while young, before it becomes hard, and continues a considerable time in use. It is well adapted for cottage culture.

Early Sugar-Loaf is a very distinct sort. The heads are perfectly conical, the leaves erect and spoon-shaped. The heads are not so firm as those already noticed, but, unless for variety, it is not desirable, as the hot weather destroys its quality.

Early Dutch is a variety that connects the more early sorts with the Drumhead. Spring-sown seed will be fit to cut in August and September, and for the table is the only desirable variety of the late sorts.

Flat Dutch, or Drumhead.—Hundreds of acres of this Cabbage are cultivated in this vicinity for city use and shipping to southern ports. They are sold at about $2,50 per 100. It is a large spreading Cabbage, generally very broad and flat at the top; of a close and firm nature. It comes to perfection about the middle of September, and will continue till January. Seed sown in May will come into use in October and continue till February.

Bergen is also a Drumhead variety, larger and coarser than the former. It is most eligible for feeding cattle or making sauer kraut.

Savoy Cabbage.—There are four varieties of this Cabbage, but the Curled and Drumhead will suffice for our purpose. *The Curled Savoy* is a delightful Winter vegetable, improved in flavor by a considerable frost. It does not head firm, but the whole of the head is fit for the kitchen. *Drumhead Savoy* grows to a large size, nearly round, and a little flattened at the top. It is the principal sort for the market; like large cabbages it fills the eye, but the Curled is the best for family use; it pleases the taste

Red Dutch.—This sort is esteemed principally as a choice pickle, and is sometimes sliced in salad. In its raw state it is of middle size, heart-shaped, heading very hard, and the whole of a red, purplish color. The darker the color, and the more thick and fleshy the leaves, without any white in the ribs and veins, the more valuable. It is in perfection from October till Christmas.

All these sorts of Cabbage are biennial, being raised from seed and attaining perfection the first year; and in the second shooting up the stalk, to flower and seed, after which they wholly perish.

To save for Seed.—Onthe approach of Winter bury the roots and stems with a part of the Cabbage, slantingly, in the ground, and in severe weather cover the heads lightly with straw. When Spring comes uncover them, and, as the stems grow, tie them up to prevent their being destroyed by the wind. The seed will ripen in June or July. Clean it, and put away in a dry place for use. If two varieties of the Brassica tribe are saved for seed in the same year, they should be in the extreme parts of the garden, or they will undoubtedly mix and degenerate.

Culture.—Fortunately the Cabbage can be cultivated by the most simple and easy means. It grows in most soils and produces its beneficial heads nine months in the year. The ground must be rich, or made so by a good coat of manure, as they have strong tapering roots. Digging or plowing deep is very essential. Indeed, this is too much neglected in the culture of all culinary crops.

To produce a constant succession of Cabbages, three principal sowings are necessary. For the early Spring and Summer crops, sow the seeds of the York, Nonpareil, Battersea and Vanack from the 12th to the 25th of September; each sort separately, on a bed of light, rich earth. Sow moderately thick, broad-cast, or over the ground, if the weather be dry. Tramp in the seed with the feet; rake evenly and smoothly, and finish by giving the beds a gentle beat with the back of the spade. If drought continues, water them a few times, and they will be up in eight or ten days. Towards the end of October, the strongest plants of this sowing will be fit to plant out. Prepare some rich, well-dug ground; draw deep drills, eighteen inches apart, and dibble the plants one foot apart in the row, on the south or east side of the drills, so as the plants may have all the benefit of the Winter suns, and be sheltered by the tops of the drills from the north and north-west winds. After the frost sets in severely, lay straw thinly across the drills, which will fully protect the plants. On the approach of Spring, remove it; these plants will be ready for cutting eight or ten days earlier than those that have been kept in frames *all Winter*. The balance of the plants for the main crop must be protected in a cold frame, covered with boards or shutters, removable at pleasure. It may be made by any person, merely taking a few boards about one foot wide; stretch them along in any sheltered situation, to the extent that will hold the required plants of Cabbages and Lettuces (say twenty feet long and six feet wide, which will hold four thousand plants, which, after allowing a considerable portion for failing, will be enough for a large family). Sink in the ground short posts of cedar or locust at back and front, and nail firmly thereto sound boards of oak or pine, the board at the back one foot high, the one on the front six inches; this, when covered, will allow the rain to run off. Throw up the earth close round the outside of the frame, to keep the water from entering under the boards or among the plants. If they are kept wet during Winter they will die off, or what gardeners call "damp off." In fact, the dryer they are kept the more safe they will be. Give air in all clear weather during Winter. In severe frost they should remain covered all day, but expose them fully in mild weather. Take care that mice do not prey upon them

If they do, take as much arsenic as will lie on a ten cent piece, mix it with a table-spoonful of Indian meal, and lay it on a piece of tile or board in the frame, where it will be dry, which will soon destroy them. Early in Spring, transplant to the compartments of the garden designed for them. Lift the plants carefully with a trowel, retaining as many fibres and soil as possible. The plants should all be assorted, planting the strongest where the crop is expected to be earliest, so that all may come to maturity regularly. In their subsequent growth, if any fail or run to seed, supply the deficiencies with fresh plants. As the crop progresses, hoe frequently and deep; destroy every weed, and as the plants grow, draw earth round the stems, which will strengthen and forward them. The large Late Yorks require the same care and treatment. They will mature in succession, according to the lateness of the sort. Where a supply of plants has not been obtained in the Fall, it will be necessary to sow seed on a hot-bed about the middle of February—for the management of which see the article CUCUMBER—only the hot-bed will not require to be so strong, and a greater portion of air admitted to the frame in sunshine, and even a small portion at night when there is no frost, gradually hardening them as they grow, till they become fit for planting out, which will be about the end of March or first of April. I have seen, however, where the garden depended upon the exertions of the cook, or the dexterous management of the housewife, a good crop of early Cabbage plants grown in the kitchen window. It is a lamentable fact that many of our otherwise industrious farmers would have no vegetables were it not for the exertions of the female portion of the family. The health and comfort of a family would be greatly enhanced by giving a full portion of attention to the manuring and cropping of a vegetable garden. It is absolutely necessary in this country, that every farmer should be a gardener, and every gardener a farmer.

For the late Summer, Fall, and Winter supply sow the seed

from the first of April to the first of May, as directed for the September sowing. The sorts are Early Dutch, Drumhead. Bergen, Savoys, and Red Dutch; sow also a few large York They will come in July or August, and be found useful for filling up vacant ground or patching. Transplanting may be in May, June, and July, as circumstances will admit. When planting out in Summer, as the weather is frequently very dry and hot, the ground should be fresh dug, the plants carefully lifted (having given them a copious watering the evening previous), and their roots dipped into a puddle or mush of cow dung, soot, or earth, before planting; then dibble them in firmly, give a good watering, and a certain growth will follow. The rows may be two feet apart, and eighteen inches from plant to plant. The after culture the same as directed for early Cabbage. When Cabbage heads have been cut, the stumps should be dug up every week and deposited in the rubbish heap. It is waste to allow them to sprout and grow, or decay and evaporate in the air. Some seasons, the fly (a small black beetle) destroys the plants as soon as they appear above the ground. Soot, air-slacked lime, and wood ashes sprinkled over them, is in part a preventive. Others destroy them by having a hen cooped, allowing the young chickens to have free access to the plants, from which they exterminate the flies. I invariably grow my scarce seed in boxes elevated eighteen inches above the ground, entirely out of the reach of this insect, which does not appear on elevated objects. This operation requires more attention in watering, but a certainty is always gained by it.

WINTERING CABBAGE—If you have not a dry, airy, vegetable cellar, nor an open shed to spare for burying them, take a sheltered part of the garden and bury the roots, stalk, and part of the head in the earth, over which, in severe weather place a few boards, or a light sprinkling of straw. In Southern latitudes this is unnecessary; there they can withstand the climate. *Coleworts*, a small kind of Cabbage, of a very tender nature and delicate flavor, can be successfully cultivated as directed for early Cabbage. Where the Winters are not severe, they, with Broccoli and Brussels sprouts, can be had for use the whole season.

CARDOON.

Cy'nara Cardŭnculus.—Cardon, Fr.—*Kardonen*, Ger.

The Cardoon is somewhat like the Artichoke, but rises to a greater height, and, with it, may be classed as one of the fanciful vegetables, grown exclusively for the name, or to please the fancy of some professed epicure. At least it has but little nutriment; the tender stalks, after being blanched, are either stewed or put in soups or salads during Autumn and Winter.

Culture.—This is easily accomplished, by sowing the seeds about the middle of Spring, where they are to remain. They succeed in soils of a sandy loam, inclining to moisture, well enriched by manure. Plant the seeds in a row six inches apart and one inch deep. When they come up, thin them out to one foot apart, as they require room to grow four feet wide and five feet high. Keep clean from weeds, hoe deep and frequently. About the beginning of October, when the plants have attained their full size, they should be prepared for blanching; choose a dry day, and tie the leaves of the plant carefully and lightly together with matting or small hay-bands. previously removing all the damaged or decayed ones; keeping the whole upright, binding the plant closely round with twisted straw or hay-bands, from the root to about two-thirds of its height, covering it so as to prevent the earth from coming in contact with the ribs of the leaves; then earth them up the height of the bands, as directed for Celery. In three weeks they will be sufficiently blanched for use, when they may be taken up as wanted. In severe weather protect them as directed for Celery.

CARROT.

Daúcus Caròta.—Carótte, Fr.—*Mohre*, Ger.

"The Carrot," says an eminent physician, "is a most wholesome culinary root; it strengthens and nourishes the body, and is very beneficial for consumptive persons." Carrots are generally served to table boiled, with meats; they make an excellent ingredient in soup, and form an agreeable pudding. As an agricultural root, they are not surpassed for feeding cattle. Horses will do more work and look better on them than on any other feed. It is supposed to have been introduced into Europe from the island of Crete, since which they have been greatly improved. The following are the leading varieties cultivated for supplying the kitchen regularly at all seasons of the year.

Early Horn is the most forward in ripening, and the best adapted for early crops, and in my opinion the best adapted for any crop. Although they are shorter than the other sorts, they require a less depth of soil, and can be grown much closer together. Its peculiar character is, the tap-root drawing abruptly off to a point. It is higher colored when pure, and sweeter in taste than the other varieties, and can be sown as late as the 20th of July. I have this year a very excellent crop sown on the 28th of July, after the Onion crop was taken from the ground.

Long Orange is the sort generally grown for a Winter crop. It is paler in color than the former, and grows to a great length, frequently two feet long.

Altringham is a bright red variety, peculiar in having from one to two inches of the top above ground. I consider this in flavor next to the Early Horn. It is excellent for a general crop, being a fine keeper for Winter use.

Long Surrey.—This variety is but imperfectly known here.

It is like the *Long Orange*, but of a brighter color. In soil of a deep sandy loam, it produces a heavy crop, and is very suitable for the Farm.

Long White is much cultivated by the French for seasoning and for soups. On light, deep soils, it produces a heavy crop.

Culture.—In the culture of this excellent vegetable, a deep, light, rich, sandy soil, well manured, should if possible be employed. If the ground is not of this quality in the preceding year, it should be dug deep, and well broken. If this is not done, the roots fork or spread in a lateral direction, injuring both their size and quality. It is very important to have an early crop, for such the *Horn* sort only should be used. Sow on a warm border, as early as the season will admit. In sowing, a calm day should be preferred, as the seeds are very light; they also bundle together, and should be rubbed between the hands in dry sand or earth, to separate them. The preferable way of sowing, is in shallow drills, half an inch deep, and nine to twelve inches apart, which admits of the hoe being made use of in thinning out the crop, and clearing off the weeds. As soon as the plants are up, and can be easily observed. take a hoe of three or four inches broad, and thin out the crop to three or four inches apart. The main crop intended for large roots, should be thinned to six inches apart. Frequent hoeing and stirring the soil, whether there are weeds to destroy or not, is very essential to the growth of the roots. From the first of May to the first of June, is the period to sow for a general crop, which will be ready to house about the first of November. As soon as the leaves begin to turn yellow, the roots can be taken up in a dry day. Cut the tops off about an inch from the crown, and pack the roots in dry earth or sand in the cellar, for Winter use; or they may be pitted out of doors, covered with two inches of straw and a foot of earth, to keep them from frost, when they can be in use till the following April.—Beets may be kept in the same manner.

CAULIFLOWER.

Brássica oleràcea, var.—*Chou-fleur*, Fr.—*Blumenkohl*, Ger.

This very delicate vegetable was first introduced into England from the island of Cypress, about a century and a half ago. Since then it has been greatly improved by the skill of the gardener. We are inclined to believe that there are only two varieties of the Cauliflower, though there are several sorts sold in the seed-shops. The early and the late are the two, and even these have frequently very little distinctive character, where they are under the same culture; and it is somewhat curious that the Dutch prefer the English seed, and the English prefer the Dutch. We have therefore to import the seeds from both countries every year, to meet the ideas of the purchasers.

Culture.—The proper seasons for sowing the seeds are, for the early Spring or Summer crop, between the eighth and twentieth of September; and for the late Autumn crop, about the first of April. The plants, as soon as they are two inches high, should be planted out in a bed of rich, light earth, three inches apart each way, so as to grow firm and stocky to remove to their final place of growth.

For the purpose of growing them in perfection, a bed of the richest light earth, two feet deep, and one-third of it well decomposed manure, in an open exposure, sheltered from the north-west, is requisite—the whole to be surrounded with a close frame, and covered with glass or shutters. It may be prepared about the first of October, to receive the plants after the ground has fully settled, which will take two weeks. Lift the plants carefully with a trowel from where they were transplanted, and plant them eighteen inches apart each way, into the pit or frame prepared for them. Give a gentle watering to the soil round the plant; press it down firmly, and little or no more water will be required till the Spring. Between each of these, plant a Lettuce of the early Butter or Royal Cabbage sorts, that will head in February and March, and be used before the Cauliflower makes much leaf to cover the ground. It will be necessary to surround the frame with dry litter to keep out the frost, and to cover the glass or shutters with dry straw or mats in time of severe weather, observing to give plenty of air, in clear, mild days, to prevent the plants from drawing or damping off at the neck. With such treatment we have seen Cauliflowers eighteen inches in diameter, and nearly as white as snow. When they are in a growing state, they should never suffer with drought. Allow a copious supply of water—if enriched, so much the better. Soap-suds is an excellent nutritive for the growth of vegetables. In the Southern States very little protection is required. Surround the roots with dry litter, and cover the plants in severe nights with mats or branches of evergreens. Be careful to supply moisture whenever the plants demand it, which is readily observed by the drooping, of the leaves.

As many of my readers may not have seen a Cauliflower, nor know from the above what it looks like, to such we say, it is a kind of Cabbage that produces within its long, pale-green leaves, a white head, very similar to a basin rounded full of the curd which is commonly called Cottage Cheese. This is about as plain a description of the appearance of this vegetable as we can give. In cutting Cauliflowers, the head should be cut off with some inches of the stalk, together with most of the surrounding leaves, which should be trimmed down nearly to the circumference of the head, when for present use; but the leaves of those required to be kept a few days, or intended for market, should be retained in their full length. If the flowers are opening more rapidly than demand requires, they can be, retarded a few days, by folding the leaves over the heads. By this process, the flower is kept of a purer white, being defended from the sun.

CELERY.

A'pium graveòlens.—*Celeri*, Fr.—*Sellerie*, Ger.

THE Celery is a native of Britain, and is found in marshy ground, ditches, and such situations. In its wild state, it has a rank, coarse taste. The effect of cultivation is remarkably displayed in producing the sweet, crisp, mild, stalk of Celery, generally very palatable to all, from a wild, detestable, and apparently worthless weed.

This vegetable is yearly gaining repute, and is cultivated to a great extent, though in our market far from being in perfection.

USE.—The leaf-stalks, when blanched, are used raw as a salad; they are also stewed, and used for seasoning soups; an agreeable conserve can also be made from the stalks when perfectly blanched.

There are several sorts in cultivation, but they may be set aside to give place to the two following:—

White Solid, which is most generally prefered, on account of the color, and is considered by some as the most crisp; and

Red Solid, which differs from the former only in color, though it withstands the frost better than the White, showing, at least, that there is a constitutional difference. *Manchester Red* is another name for this variety. There are also sorts sold as Giant Red and Giant White, Seymour's Red and Seymour's White, all corresponding with the varieties known as the Red and White Solid Celery. There is another variety known as the Lion's-Paw Celery, pure white, but in our opinion inferior to the White Solid. As for giant sorts, they are attained purely by culture, and astonishingly so too. Seed from the same plant, in the hands of some growers, will produce stalks four feet long, blanched to a silvery whiteness; with others, a meagre stalk of a few inches high, with its base of a dirty rusty, greenish-white—which, of course, will be pronounced an inferior sort, and the blame attached to the seed.

CULTURE.—To procure early Celery, the seed should be sown on a gentle hot-bed, from the first to the middle of March Collect a load or two of warm horse-manure. Put it in a form eighteen inches thick, to be covered with a frame and glass sash. When the violent heat has subsided, cover it with six inches of light soil, whereon sow your seed. Press it down, and rake it lightly, giving a gentle watering. Put on the glasses; shade from severe sun; give a little air from 11 to 2 o'clock; and as soon as the plants are up, air freely. Thin them out to half an inch apart. When they are three inches high, plant them out into a well-prepared bed of rich, light soil, which will be from the first to the middle of April—cover at night with mats or boards, to protect from cold or frost. By the first of June, they will be sufficiently strong to plant out in trenches for blanching. However, where extreme earliness is not an object, sow the seed about the first of April, on a rich, dry, warm border; when up, thin them out. About the middle of May, transplant them, three or four inches apart, into another piece of ground, to stock and harden, till they are finally planted into the rows for permanent culture.

The regular way is to select a level and rich piece of ground; dig the trenches a foot wide, ten inches deep, and three feet from each other; if convenient, from north to south, though any other aspect will do. Let the earth be regularly thrown out on each side of the trench, and sloped off. Five or six inches of well decomposed manure should then be worked full half-spade deep into the bottom of each trench. The plants which were transplanted into the beds or frame should be carefully lifted, and prepared for planting, which is done by cutting off the extremity of the roots; shortening their tops or leaves, but not so low as to injure the young centre leaves; and divesting the neck of the plant from suckers. This done they may be planted into the trenches, at the distance of four or five inches apart; after which, give the whole a good soaking of water, and shade from the sun for a few days. Their after-culture, is to stir the soil frequently, with a small hoe, and giving a copious supply of water in continued dry weather. About the middle of August, or first of September, tie the leaves together, or hold them tight with one hand, while with the other the earth is carefully drawn up round the stems, but not so high as to allow the earth to get into the centre of the plant, which causes it to rot or rust. The soil for this purpose has to be broken, and well pulverized with the spade. If the weather be dry and hot, Celery should not be earthed up so early: in such case, a row for early use may be blanched, by placing a board on each side, and throwing the earth along the bottom edge of the board, to prevent the air from getting under. By this means it can be very well blanched, and ready for the table by the middle of September. I am aware that writers on the subject say, "earth it up every few days as it continues to grow;" but with such a practice in warm weather, it will not grow long, but rot off and decay. About the first of October, earthing up may proceed without injury; but let it be done firmly and evenly, and in a sloping direction, from the base to nearly the top of the leaves. In that state, it will remain sound for a long time. If continued frost be apprehended, dry litter should be spread over the plants, and a quantity lifted and laid in a bed of sand or earth in the vegetable cellar, in which it will keep fresh for several weeks.

When planting, it is a very convenient method to mix both Red and White together: you will thus obtain both sorts in use, from the opening of one trench. Large fields of Celery can be pretty successfully cultivated with the plough, for supplying the market. It is a crop that generally makes a good return to the grower.

Celeriac, or *Turnip-Rooted Celery*, is occasionally cultivated for its seasoning qualities, and when well boiled is used at the table. Culture, same as Cabbage. When the roots have acquired a tolerable size, draw the earth to each side of the row, three or four inches high, which will render them white and tender, particularly so in moist weather (the whole of this family being partial to moisture). In from four to six weeks after being earthed up, they will be in good order for use.

CHERVIL.

Scándix Cerefòlium.—*Cerfeuil*, Fr.—*Gartenkerbel*, Ger.

Is a warm, mild, and aromatic plant, a native of Europe, and in olden times of great repute. After being boiled, it was eaten with oil and vinegar, and considered a panacea for courage, comfort to the heart, and strength to the body. It is much cultivated by the French and Dutch, who use the tender leaves in soups and salads as frequently as we use Parsley, and is considered by many to be a milder and more agreeable ingredient.

Culture.—Chervil is an annual plant, and should be sown in March, April, and May, in drills, about a quarter of an inch deep, and nine inches apart. Cover lightly, and press the soil firm with the foot, rake evenly, and give a gentle watering in dry weather. The leaves are fit for use, when two to four inches high. Cut them off close; they will come up again, and may be gathered in succession throughout the season.

CHIVE.

A'llium Schænŏprassum.—*Civette*, Fr.—*Binsenlauch*, Ger.

Allium is the botanical generic name for all roots of the Onion family, to which this belongs. It is a British plant and is supposed to partake of the flavor of both the Onion and the Leek. Its principal use is for soups and salads. The fine rush-like leaves, when about three or four inches high, are fit for use. They grow again with surprising rapidity, and are the earliest Spring salad, or seasoning.

Culture.—It is a hardy perennial bulb, and, when once planted, will continue to grow for many years in any soil. They make very good edgings for any compartment of the kitchen garden. Plant them in March or October, a few inches apart, and two inches deep: they will soon spread into a large bush, and not suffer in the extremest cold.

CORN SALAD.

Fédia olitória.—Mache, Fr.—*Ackersalat*, Ger.

Fetticus or *Lambs' Lettuce* is a native of Europe, and cultivated extensively as a Spring salad, but in France they frequently dress it like Spinach. It is called Lambs' Lettuce, from its having been in repute as an early feed for lambs. Every garden should have a patch of this very palatable vegetable, as it comes early in Spring, when even the sight of green is refreshing.

Culture.—Sow the seed from the 8th to the 20th of September, in shallow drills, one-fourth inch deep and six inches apart: cover lightly, and if dry weather, tread or roll the ground to press the seed and soil together. It is an annual, and requires to be sown every year. Hoe and keep clear of weeds; in November cover slightly with straw; when wanted, the leaves should be picked and not cut. If the Winter proves mild, it will be in use the whole season. If the seed is not fresh every year, it will frequently lie six months in the ground before it vegetates. It requires good rich soil; on such the flavor is greatly improved.

CRESS.

Lepidium Sativum—Cresson, Fr.—*Kresse*, Ger.

Curled or Pepper Cress takes its name from its warm, spicy, pungent flavor. It is very generally cultivated as an early salad. In Europe it is daily on the tables of the wealthy, and can be grown fit for use on a warm hot-bed in forty-eight hours.

Culture.—The seed should always be sown on very rich, light ground, that it may grow as rapidly as possible, being cut while perfectly young and in a crisp state. It is fully ready when one inch high, and is best when only once cut, though many allow it to get two or three inches high, cutting off only the tops and allowing it to grow for repeated croping. To have it very early, sow in February on a gentle hot-bed, where the glass can be placed within a few inches of the soil. The sowings in the open ground begin about the end of March, and should be continued every week for two months. Sow the seed very thick, either in drills or broad cast; earth over very lightly, just enough to cover the seed; and press it even with the back of the spade. In dry weather give occasional waterings. In cold nights cover the ground with mats, or straw, to ward off any frost. When grown in hot-beds, give plenty of air during the day. A family can use from four ounces to a pound of seed.

CUCUMBER.

Cucumis Sativus.—Concombre, Fr.—*Gurke*, Ger.

The Cucumber is a fruit of great antiquity, found wild in all warm countries, and is cultivated to an amazing extent all over the world—a surprising fact, when contrasted with its nourishing qualities, few or none of our culinary vegetables having less nutriment, it being of a cold and watery nature, and to persons of a weak and delicate constitution very indigestive. When dressed with oil, vinegar, and pepper, it is freely used to cool the feelings and sharpen the appetite: hence the common saying, "as cool as a cucumber." Of the many sorts in cultivation, we select the following, as being dissimilar, and worthy of culture, either for the frame or open air.

Early Short White Prickly.—Fruit from four to six inches long, of a sea-green color, with white spines; forces very well, and is grown extensively for market. It does not get yellow so soon as the *Early Short Prickly*, which is of the same size, of a dark green color, with black spines.

Long Early Frame.—This is used both for forcing and open air culture. It grows from six to ten inches long, a good bearer and a very excellent variety.

Manchester Prize.—Dark green, with black spines. An English variety; of great excellence either as a fruit or abundant bearer; generally grown in the gardens of the wealthy about Philadelphia, and is often seen at our Exhibitions twenty inches to two feet long.

Kerrison's Long White Spine, in size and form similar to the former. The spines or prickles are white: a good bearer.

Long Prickly grows about ten inches long; dark-green color, black prickles; a great bearer. This variety, with the two first named, are the most certain for general crops; the other long sorts are equally as crisp, if not more so, but they are not so plentiful bearers, neither do they produce seed in any quantity. If different sorts of Cucumbers are grown contiguous to each other, they are certain to mix, and the seed from them will not produce the genuine variety. There are also white Cucumbers, and white with black spines, but their taste is flatter and more insipid.

CULTURE in the open air is of the simplest character

Merely dig out a hole, about a foot wide and deep; fill it with rich, sandy soil; raise it above the surface about six inches: the hills should be six feet apart each way. Any time in May, sow a few seeds therein, and the result is certain. If the weather be warm, they will grow in a few days; if the nights are cold, protect them. There is frequently a little bug, which preys upon the tender leaves; if so, soot and wood ashes sprinkled over them, while wet with the dew, will retard the progress of the depredator. As soon as the vines have made three rough leaves, nip the points off to make them branch out. They will fruit sooner by it. Three vines to one hill is quite enough. To have young fruit in February and March is rather a nice operation, but any one who can command a few loads of warm horse-manure, can have them from April to October. That farmers in the country may have the article either for family use or for sale, a few hints may be in place on

Forcing Cucumbers.—The first requisite is to obtain four feet square of warm stable-manure; turn it up into a heap for eight or ten days, to allow the rank vapor to pass off, when it may be placed into any form to suit a sash. The general size is four by six feet, and three or four feet high at the back, sloping to two and a half or three feet at front. Either make or have made a frame of boards, at least fifteen inches deep, three feet wide, and five feet long, or the full size of the sash. Let the dung-bed be a foot all round larger than the frame. Should heavy rain or snow fall, or it be a severe frost, the manure should be protected with a covering of straw. Care, however, should always be taken that the reduction of the heat in the dung is not carried too far, before making up the bed, as, when that is the case, too little heat will afterwards be produced, and the young plants will be of a yellow color instead of a rich green. The bed should be built square up, and regularly beaten down with the fork. When finished, put on the frame and sash; keep it close for a day or two, to draw up the heat; air should then be admitted for a few days, during the day, by tilting up the sash at the back a few inches, to allow the steam to pass off, which it generally does in four or five days or less. Supposing the bed now in order, put in a quantity (three barrow-loads) of light, rich loam: none better than that from the surface of the woods. In two or three days the earth will be sufficiently warm for sowing the seeds. If the plants are to be removed into other frames, sow them in pots; if not to be removed, sow them in a hill made in the centre of the bed, by placing one barrow-full more of earth in it. Sow a few dozen seeds to meet contingencies, or any extra supply, in pots, in case of damping off—which frequently happens in cloudy Winter weather. Cover the sash at night with straw mats, or any similar protection, and surround the bed with litter or boards, to keep the piercing winds from carrying off the heat. The seed should be two or three years old; (it is better than new seed, which goes more to vine than fruit.) It will be up in twenty-four hours, and in two or three days will grow into strong plants. During their growth, admit fresh air every day at the back; give the young plants as much light as possible; when they have attained their third rough leaf, nip the point off the vine, to cause it to branch. If the soil or the plants appear to be dry, give them water in the forenoon, which has been kept in the bed during the previous night, that it may be in a warm state. The plants succeed best when they are transplanted, and plant them deep enough for the earth to reach to their seed-leaves. As the plants grow, roots will protrude from their stems, to which earth may be drawn. The roots will also appear through the hill, to which a farther supply of fresh soil may be added When the plants have grown and the sun is very warm, they may flag or droop: if so, sprinkle a few straws or a very thin mat on the glass, right over them, about mid-day; but it is best to grow them without this precaution; and it is unnecessary when they have sufficient moisture, heat, and depth of soil. The requisite temperature is from 65° to 75°, and from 75° to 100° by day Experience can manage these affairs with sight and feeling, but the untutored require the aid of a thermometer and a stick to poke into the dung-bed, to ascertain the internal heat of the material. When it begins to decline, give it a fresh lining of manure all around, of eighteen inches in thickness, and as high as to cover half of the frame. The vines, if well managed, will bloom within a month from the day of sowing. The male and female flowers are on the same plant, and art may render assistance, by taking the male blossom and putting its centre within the female, which is easily distinguished by having at its base a form of a cucumber, half an inch long. After being impregnated, it will be fit to cut in two weeks. These operations may be begun and gone through any time from Christmas to March. To cultivate cucumbers extensively, all that is requisite is a preparation of manure, frames, and sash. Use the above described bed for growing the seedling plants, transplanting them into larger frames or pits, (see fig. 15,) three plants being sufficient for each sash, and fifty to seventy fruit may be cut from each light. When the author was gardener to the late Henry Pratt, Esq., of Lemon Hill, near this city, he cut Cucumbers in February, and had them for the table regularly till they could be obtained from the open ground.

Cucumbers can also be cultivated under hand-glasses; (see Fig. 13.) Dig out a pit early in April, eighteen inches deep and wide, fill it with warm manure, and cover with six or eight inches of rich light soil, in which sow the seed. Hand-glasses are made of various sizes, but such as are eighteen inches square will be found the most useful. Admit air during sunshine, as directed for frames, and if cold nights prevail, cover them with mats or litter of any kind. Cucumbers for pickling should be sown from the end of June to the 15th of July. Either the Short Prickly or Long Green is suitable for the purpose. There is also a small Cluster Cucumber used by some for bottling or mixing with a finer sort of pickles.

Where Cucumbers are grown for family use, it is of great advantage to cover the ground with straw, which will keep the sun from parching the soil in hot, dry weather, and prevent the blossoms and young fruit from being covered with soil during heavy rains.

EGG-PLANT.

Solănum Melongĕna.—Melongene, Fr.—*Tollapfel,* Ger.

The Egg-Plant was introduced from Africa, and is called by some the Guinea Squash. It is generally cultivated, and becoming more so every year. They are cut into thin slices and fried, and have a taste very similar to oysters. Others use them in stews and soups. They are fit for the kitchen when they attain the size of a goose egg, and are in use till they become nearly ripe, which is easily known by the seeds changing to a brown color. Many individuals are exceedingly fond of them, while others will not taste them in any form. The following varieties are cultivated:

Large Prickly-Stemmed Purple grows larger than any of the varieties, and is frequently seen two feet in circumference; shape, oval; color, dark purple.

Smooth-Stemmed, so called because it has no prickles on the stem, does not grow so large as the former. Shape, long oval; color, dark shining purple; a few days earlier than the Prickly.

Long Purple is considered by some superior in flavor to either of the former; it is eight to ten days earlier, a very prolific variety, and the best for family use.

White Egg-Plant.—The name Egg Plant is taken from this variety, which is, when in a half-grown state, very like a hen's egg in shape, color, and size.

Culture.—There is a great ambition among growers to have this vegetable in early use. I delight to encourage this emulation whenever it is manifested. Competition promotes industry, and industry promotes health. Man possessing these ingredients is very rarely unhappy. Sow the seeds on a gentle hot-bed about the first of March, on a rich, light soil; give a good watering, and keep the frame close for a few days till the seed comes up. Be careful to give the soil a sprinkling of water whenever it appears to be dry. As soon as the plants grow, give air freely, covering the glass in cold nights. When they attain the height of two inches, thin them out to three inches apart, or transplant them into another bed. Where there is plenty of room, the latter is the best method. They can be transplanted out from the 1st to the 15th of May, into a warm border of rich ground, from whence the early Lettuce or Radishes have been taken. Give a good watering after being removed; hoe well; keep clean; as they grow draw earth to their stems. They will cut about the end of June or 1st of July. For a late crop, sow in April, on a warm border where they are to remain, or transplant in June during moist weather. Plant in rows two feet apart, and two feet from plant to plant. The seed will keep three or four years. Sow Valentine Beans between the rows.

ENDIVE.

Chicòrium Endívia.—*Chicorèe*, Fr.—*Endivie*, Ger.

The Garden Endive is a native of northern China, and has been cultivated in Europe the past three centuries for a Winter salad. The French are particularly fond of it, using it raw, pickled, fried and boiled, esteeming it exceedingly wholesome in every form, and agreeing with every constitution. There are four varieties, which we will name in the order we esteem them.

Green Curled has beautiful curled or lancinated leaves. It is a fine stocky and hardy variety, is the principal sort for salads, and when well cultivated, is very beautiful.

Broad-Leaved has a plain, thick leaf, slightly wrinkled, and turning inwards; it is preferred for stews and soups.

White Curled is rather a delicate variety, and cannot well be carried through the Winter; its principal use is therefore for the early Autumn crop. It will blanch in a few days.

Batavian is a broad, plain-leaved sort, principally cultivated for cooking, and makes a fine head.

Culture.—For the early crop, sow about the first of July. It will do on the ground where early Cabbage or Peas have come off, by giving it a coat of manure. Draw drills the depth of the hoe, one foot apart, and sow therein; sprinkle a little earth in the bottom of the drill sufficient to cover the seed, which will be up in a few days. If dry weather ensue, water once or twice till the plants get hold. Thin them out when about two inches high to ten inches apart; hoe freely, and keep clear of weeds. Being grown in these shallow drills, they are more easily earthed up and grow better in warm, dry weather. When the leaves have attained about eight inches long they are fit for blanching; for this purpose a dry day must be chosen. Gather up the leaves in your hand, in a close and rounded form; see that there is no earth or litter in their centre; tie them up with a piece of cotton-twist or mating, which is to go several times round the plant, causing it to close at the top to prevent the rain from penetrating to and injuring its centre; then draw a little earth round its base for support. If the leaves are not perfectly dry when tied up, they will rot, or become so stained as to be unfit for the table. They will take about ten days in warm and twenty days in cool weather to blanch for use; a judgment may thus be formed of the quantity to be tied up at a time. For late crops, sow about the end of July. If the ground is not ready, they may be sown in a bed and transplanted during moist weather, giving a few waterings if the season be dry. To have it in perfection through Winter, it should be planted in frames in August and allowed to grow there; or removed from the ground into the frames about the first of November, lifting a portion of soil with their roots. Keep them rather dry during Winter, as they are liable to damp off; cover with shutters or sash; sprinkle a few dry leaves among the plants and tie them up as demand requires. Give plenty of air in sunshine or mild weather; they require protection only from heavy rains and severe frosts. *Observe*, the leaves must not be tied up when they are in a frozen state. They may also be blanched by covering them with a pot of any description, which is often used as a precautionary method in Winter.

FENNEL.

Anèthum Fœnículum.—*L'Aneth*, Fr.—*Dillkraut*, Ger.

Is a native of Europe, and may be seen growing wild on the banks of rivers and near the sea coasts. It is an indispensable ingredient in French cookery, and extensively used by the English, but comparatively in little demand with us. Its tender stalks are used in soups and fish sauces, also as garnishes for dishes. It is conspicuous as a medicinal plant, and admitted into the Materia Medica; its virtues are stomachic and carminative.

Culture.—Fennel is cultivated by sowing the seeds early in Spring, in shallow drills half an inch deep and ten inches wide, covering with fine earth. They should be sown where they are intended to grow. Thin out the plants to four inches apart; a dozen of good roots will supply any family, and when once established, there is little fear of losing it, being a perennial and will last many years. Seedlings will also come up plentifully around the old plants, though it is not advisable to allow the plants to go to seed unless it is wanted for use. If the flower stems are cut off as soon as they appear, it will encourage a production of young leaves below.

GARLIC.

Al'lium Sativum.—Ail, Fr.—*Knoblauch,* Ger.

THE term Garlic is given to this vegetable on account of its powerful and penetrating scent. It is a native of many parts of the world, and has been in general use for two centuries. Many very excellent and medicinal qualities are attributed to its root, and it would no doubt be more generally used if it were not for its unpleasant odor. The French use it in sauces and salads.

CULTURE.—There are two varieties cultivated, under the name of Large and Small. As either of them is large enough for any purpose, one variety only is necessary. The root is bulb, divided into parts called psuedo-bulbs or cloves. It is propagated by planting these cloves in drills two inches deep, six inches apart, and four inches from plant to plant, early in Spring, on light, rich ground. It requires to be frequently hoed and kept free from weeds. About the end of July the bulbs are generally full grown, which will be evident from the yellow appearance and withering of the leaves. They must then be taken up, cleaned and dried, and afterwards tied in bundles, to be hung up in a shed or room and preserved for use.

HORSE-RADISH.

Cochleària armoràcia.—Cranson, Fr.—*Merrettig,* Ger.

HORSE-RADISH is a native of Europe, growing in deep soil and marshy places. It has been long cultivated in our gardens either for medicine, salads, or sauces. The root, scraped into shreds, or grated fine and soaked in vinegar, is a well-known accompaniment to roast beef. Its medicinal effects are to stimulate the glands to activity; and on account of its warm nature it is good in numerous cases arising from cold and viscid juices. The root, when fresh grated, assists digestion; it may therefore be properly employed as a condiment at the table. It is also considered of great service in rheumatic cases, and on the first appearance of scurvy.

Culture.—In a commercial point of view it has become of late extensively cultivated; acres are yearly planted and allowed to grow two or three years, when it is lifted and sold by weight to pickle manufacturers, who grind it up, and pack it in jars with vinegar for home use and exportation. It grows best in a deep, rich soil, inclining to moisture; on low ground, or contiguous to water. It is propagated by the tops or crowns, or any part of the root cut into pieces two inches long will grow.

When a convenient spot of ground is chosen, take out an opening at one end fifteen inches deep, in the common way of trenching, and two feet wide. Plant therein two rows, one foot apart and nine inches from plant to plant. Put over them from the next trench fifteen inches of soil, and so continuing till the whole is finished.

Another method of planting is readily done by trenching the ground as above, and leveling and raking it properly. Then take a dibber fifteen inches long, and of sufficient thickness to allow the sets to drop into the bottom of the holes so made, and fill up the holes with fine earth. This method makes a very clean and handsome root. To make the most of every part of the Garden, some light and quick crop may be sown on the ground early in Spring after being planted, such as Spinach, Radish, Lettuce, &c., which will be off in time not to injure the roots. As Spring has its multitude of operations, we recommend the Horse-radish to be planted in November. When the roots are required for use, open a trench on one side of the row, then clear the plants down to the roots from whence they spring, and cut them off, leaving a small portion to form another plant the following season, though it is decidedly preferable to make a new plantation every two years, as when the roots become old they have a hard, bitter taste. Before the Winter sets in, there should be a sufficient supply lifted for use, and stored in the root-cellar, in moist earth. If they are allowed to become dry, they lose their sprightly flavor

---

INDIAN CORN.

Zéa Màys.—Mais, Fr.

THIS vegetable is universally cultivated for the table throughout the United States. Its varieties are numerous, and yearly increasing. Those particularly adapted for the table have been greatly improved the past few years. It is an indispensable dish for both the rich and the poor, in its season. By a knowledge of its culture, and attention to repeated sowings, it may be had from June to November. The following three varieties are the best for the purpose:

Extra Early.—This is the earliest variety; grains large and pure white, cob small, ears short; if planted from the 15th to 25th of April, it will be ready about the same days in June; but when planted about the 15th of May, it will be ready about the 1st of July, if the weather is favorable.—Fine flavored.

Adams' Early—very similar to the above, but a few days later. Grains not so full though equally as fine flavored.

Sweet, or *Sugar.*—There are two varieties of this; the one that has eight rows of grains on the cob is the best. It remains some time in a milky state, and therefore the same sowing is fit for the table a longer period. The grains of the

Sugar Corn, when in a dry state, are small and shriveled, and are consequently easily distinguished.

Culture.—The ground must be in good condition; if not make it so, or put a shovelful of decayed manure or rich compost into each hill. Plant in hills, three feet apart, five or six grains in each; when up, allow three only to stand for a crop; hoe deep and frequently, drawing some earth to the stalks when about a foot high. If they incline to sucker, or make side shoots, break them off. Plant every two weeks till August. This crop can be used to fill up all vacancies in the ground, and to follow other crops as they come off in June and July.

INDIAN CRESS, OR NASTURTIUM.

Tropæolum màjus.—*Capucine*, Fr.—*Kapuzinerblume*, Ger.

The botanic name is derived from a Latin word signifying a warlike trophy. This idea might have originated with botanists from its shield-like leaves and its brilliant, golden, helmet-shaped flowers, pierced and stained with blood. It is a native of Peru and Chili, where there are many curious and fanciful varieties, though none so beautiful as the *Common Nasturtium* that has been cultivated for nearly three hundred years. Its gay colors enliven the gardens of the rich and the poor. The flowers and leaves have a sharp and warm taste, like Garden or Curled Cress; and are frequently used in salads. The seeds, when gathered young and green, on a dry day, and pickled in vinegar, form an excellent substitute for Capers, and indeed are *preferable.*

Culture.—It is properly treated as an annual plant, and sown for the benefit of its seed, flowers and foliage, as well as for ornament. Sow the seed thinly, in rows or patches, an inch deep, about the end of March or first of April. It is not particular in regard to either soil or situation; they will thrive almost any where, if the ground is rich. The plants will run from five to fifteen feet, and require stakes or trellis-work to climb upon. They are excellent for a blind, to cover any disagreeable object There are several varieties of yellow, golden, or crimson color. The yellow stands the severity of the sun better than the crimson.

JERUSALEM ARTICHOKE.

Heliánthus Tuberósus.—Poire de Terre, Fr.—*Erde Apfel*, Ger.

THE tuberous-rooted Sunflower, as the name implies, is a native of South America, and has been cultivated for two centuries. Like many other new vegetables, when first introduced, it was extolled extravagantly. It was baked in pies, with dates, ginger, raisins, &c.; and of course amalgamated with such good things that it could not taste indifferently. When boiled in the simple way of Potatoes, however, they will not form a very palatable dish. The modern way of serving them up, is to boil them till they become tender, when, after being peeled and stewed with butter and wine, they are considered pleasant, and taste similar to the true Artichoke. They are not so good as Potatoes, but, as a crop for feeding hogs or cattle, they are more productive.

CULTURE.—They are propagated and planted in the same manner as the Potatoe, any time in March, and will grow in any soil, even under trees. They are best fresh planted every year, and require good, light ground. The stems grow to eight or ten feet high, and have the appearance of the Sunflower. They are in use from October to April. Any time in November, a quantity may be lifted and packed away in sand or earth, for Winter use: or cover the ground with rough litter, to keep out severe frost, and they can be lifted as required. The frost does not injure the tubers.

LEEK.

Al'lium Pórrum—Porreau, Fr.—*Lauch,* Ger.

This is a branch of the Onion family, a native of the north of Europe; is very hardy, and from its mild qualities is preferred by many families to the Onion. History records it as having been cultivated many hundred years. The Welsh indulge in Leeks on their patron St. David's day, in commemoration of a victory which they obtained over the Saxons, which they attribute to the Leeks they wore by order of St. David, to distinguish them in battle. There are two varieties, the

London Leek, so called from the preference given to it in the London market. It is a strong growing variety, with the leaves all round alike.

The Scotch, or *Flag.*—So denominated from the preference given to it in the Edinburgh market, and also from the leaves being on two sides of the plant only, flag-like. They are both equally good, and either of the sorts is sufficient for a family.

Culture.—There is no part of the garden too rich for Leeks. They require the best ground, well worked and manured the full depth of the spade. Sow the seed thinly on a small bed of light, rich ground, in drills six inches apart, and half an inch deep; rake it evenly, and give it a beat with the back of the spade. When they come up, they should stand an inch apart; if thicker, thin them out. When grown to about eight inches high, they will be of sufficient size to plant out.—As we have remarked, choose the best ground, draw thereon drills a foot apart, and as deep as the hoe will go. When ready, the plants are to be taken up from the seed-bed. Shorten their roots to about an inch from the plant, and cut two inches or more from the extremity of the leaves. Both these operations are done for convenience and neatness in planting. Dibble them in the drills eight inches apart, and as deep as the plant will admit of, not to cover the young leaves pushing from its centre. Choose moist or cloudy weather for the operation; but if dry, give the plants a copious watering. Hoe the ground frequently, to keep down weeds; and as the plants are observed to grow, draw the soil around them. By good culture, they will be fit for use early in October. On the approach of severe frost, lift sufficient for Winter use, and store them away in earth or sand.

LETTUCE.

Lactŭcă satīva.—*Laitue*, Fr.—*Gartensalat*, Ger.

THIS plant is named from the Latin word *lac*, on account of the milky juice with which it abounds. It is considered very healthy, especially in the Spring of the year. There are some of the family natives of all the warm and temperate latitudes of the globe. The leading cabbaging kinds were originally introduced from Egypt; those of upright growth, from the Island of Cos: hence the name of Cos Lettuce is applied to all the sorts that approach that character. Some of the varieties have been extensively cultivated for opium preparations. The plant is allowed to shoot up till just on the eve of flowering, when the top is cut off in the afternoon. In thirty-six hours there is a brown crust found on the wounded part of the stem, which is carefully collected. The stem is again cut, and repeatedly, till the plant ceases to yield its milky substance. It is unquestionably the best of the salading vegetables. Many varieties are cultivated in Europe, and not a few in this country; but several kinds grown there are not adapted to our high and dry temperatures. The following cabbaging sorts are the best cultivated at the present time.

Brown Dutch.—Two kinds, the White and the Yellow Seeded; the latter the best; both very hardy: resists the severity of the Winter without any protection.

Early Cabbage or *White Butter*, a very early sort; does excellent for forcing on hotbeds; the leaves of a pale green; the heads white.

Royal Cabbage, a large, dark green variety; two weeks later then the former. There are two kinds of it—the White and the Black Seeded, the latter prefered. It does very well for a Summer salad, while the early Cabbage goes to seed without heading.

Drumhead is a very fine, large variety, does well in Summer, and forms a noble plant for a dish.

Green Hammersmith is a very hardy variety, heads well, and matures early.

Victoria is a new Cabbage Lettuce, that promises well, having large heads of a white, crispy nature. It appears to withstand the heat. We have only grown it one season.

White Silesia, though not so delicate in flavor as some of the former, yet is very acceptable in the heat of July, when nearly every other variety fails. It is early, hearts well, and very crisp.

Large Indian. This appears to be the only variety we have that is perfect through the whole heat of Summer; in fact, it requires heat to make it eatable, for in May and June it is much too coarse for the table, along with the other fine sorts.

The following are Cos Lettuces, all very celebrated in Europe, but with us they do not appear to retain their reputation. Our long, dry, warm Summers, prevent their coming to a crisp head; in fact, many of them never head, unless very early in the season. They should be tied up like Endive, eight or ten days before they are cut, unless they show a disposition to head.

White Cos, of strong, upright growth, stands the heat well, and if tied for ten days, blanches beautifully.

Brown or *Bath Cos*, a very hardy sort, can be cultivated under a wall or fence all Winter, when it will come to use very early in Spring.

Paris Cos, a fine variety, grows strong and upright, very crisp, and one of the best of the Cos. It is improved by tying up eight or ten days before it is cut.

Green Cos, a very hardy sort, rather coarse-growing; but when tied up a few days before being cut, it becomes much more tender.

CULTURE.—The soil best adapted for the growth of Lettuce, is a light, deep, rich, sandy loam, well worked and manured. The roots are very fibrous, and go in search of food to a great depth and breadth. Where there are only a few sorts cultivated, they will require a continued succession of sowings, but where there is a proper variety, four or five sowings in the year will keep the table well supplied. It is one of the few vegetables that can be had in perfection throughout the year, by judicious management. It is a crop too that can be introduced between other crops, without any disadvantage, by transplanting from the seed-bed on every suitable occasion. For sorts that will be in use in June, July, and August, sow Early Cabbage, Royal Cabbage, Drumhead, Silesean, and Indian, on a bed of rich, light ground, as early in March as the season will admit. Sow a few of each again about the end of April. Sow Early Cabbage, Royal Cabbage, and Victoria, in August, and about the fifteenth of September a general sowing of all the sorts. The Brown Dutch, and other heading kinds for planting in drills, to stand out all Winter, as recommended for Early York Cabbage; the Early Cabbage Lettuce, for heading in frames during Winter; and the other sorts to be transplanted into boxes, very closely, about the middle or end of October, and protected with boards or shutters during Winter, giving plenty of air every mild day. See that they are not preyed upon by slugs; if so, a dusting of air-slacked lime or soot will destroy them. They should be planted out as early in Spring as the season will admit. The varieties of the Cos Lettuce can only be successfully grown by sowing late in September, protecting them in Winter, and transplanting them out early in Spring. The seed should always be sown thinly and evenly, on fresh-dug ground, in very shallow drills, nine inches apart. Rake it smoothly, and if in dry weather, press it gently with the back of the spade. When they have grown an inch high, thin them out to two inches apart. After they begin to touch each other, give another thinning, when they can be transplanted, if required, into other compartments for a crop. As it is an article of every-day demand, a few seeds should be sprinkled in with the more permanent crops, such as Beets, Onions, Carrots, &c. Lettuce are impatient of being transplanted during warm weather; the late Spring sowings and the early Fall sowings should therefore be made where they are intended to grow, and thinned out as they advance in growth. I need scarcely add that hoeing deep and frequent is indispensable to secure a good crop. In this vicinity there are hundreds of acres of this crop planted out in October and November, on the south side of deep drills, drawn by the hoe; after the ground has become hard, these drills have straw strewn lightly across them during Winter; early in Spring it is removed, when the plants grow rapidly, head early, and are off the ground in time to plant it with Egg-plants and Tomatoes, thereby having two very profitable crops off the ground in one year.

Should it happen by accident or neglect, that there are no plants for Spring crops, recourse must be had to sowing on a slight hot-bed in February. When the plants are up, thinned out, and properly hardened, they are planted out about the end of March, or first of April, and treated as before directed. Lettuces may be had in perfection throughout the whole Winter, if planted in a sunk pit (see p. 15) or frame, early in October, and protected from frost by glass sash and straw mats, giving plenty of air during sunshine, but never allowing a draft from front to back, if there be severe frost. The earth should be within eight inches of the glass, to keep the plants as near the light as possible. The best sorts are the Early Cabbage and Royal Cabbage. Plant them eight to ten inches apart, each way, and alternately opposite. Give occasional watering, picking off all decayed leaves. If the Winter proves very severe, surround the frame or pit with dry leaves from the woods; this precaution can nearly always be conveniently adopted; leaves being everywhere plentiful, a store should always be at hand. In all the southern States, every variety of the Lettuce is perfectly hardy, and can be grown in perfection from October to May. The varieties of Cos heart freely, if tied as recommended for Endive, and are greatly benefited by that simple operation.

MARJORAM.

Origănum Majorăna.—Marjolaine, Fr.—*Marjoran,* Ger.

SWEET Marjoram is a native of the South of Europe. It has a pleasant odor, and a warm, aromatic, bitterish taste. It is used for seasoning soups, and other matters of cookery, and considered a wholesome ingredient, and beneficial in nervous complaints. There are two varieties, the Sweet and the Pot Marjoram; the former, an annual, and the latter an herbaceous plant, or a plant that lasts from year to year.

CULTURE.—Marjoram seed is of the very smallest description, and has to be sown early in April. On ground finely prepared, make a mark along the line with the point of a stick, merely to show where the seed is to be dropped, which do very thinly and evenly, then cover up with the back of the rake. The rows should be ten inches apart. As soon as the plants appear, thin them out to two inches apart. When the plant offers to bloom, cut the stems and dry them in the shade.

When dry, tie them in paper bags, and hang them up in a dry room for use. Let a few plants ripen for seed.

Pot Marjoram, or *Winter Marjoram*, is propagated by dividing the roots early in Spring and planting it in beds. Cut it when in full bloom; dry in the shade; wrap it up, and preserve it for Winter use.

MELON.

Cucumis Mèlo.—*Melon*, Fr.—*Melone*, Ger.

THE Melon, in some character, is to be found in all tropical countries, but the finest varieties are supposed to have come from Persia and Affghanistan. It has been cultivated in Europe nearly four hundred years, and in the south of that continent, in its season, it constitutes the principal part of the food of the lower classes, proving that it is both wholesome and nutricious. The *flesh* of a well-grown melon is delicious. It is eaten with ginger, pepper, sugar, salt, or as fancy and taste dictate. Its nature is cooling. There are many varieties in culture, which, with artificial aid, can be brought to perfection, but when left to unassisted nature and exposed to heavy rains and scorching suns, the number is very limited indeed. They are confined to the indifferent, or improved culture and purity of three or four sorts.

Musk Melon, so called from its peculiar scent, is nearly round; color, a yellowish green; rind smooth, and the fruit very slightly ribbed. It used to be extensively cultivated for its productive qualities, but now gives way to better varieties.

Early Cantaloupe takes its name from a village near Rome, where it has been grown for many centuries, and from thence distributed to this Western world. There are many varieties of it readily distinguished from the former by having small warts on the rind, the flesh greener, and more firm.—Well flavored.

Netted Citron is an oval fruit, roughly netted all over, of a pale yellowish green when ripe; grows to a good size; from two to five pounds; flesh, green, firm, juicy, and high flavored. This variety commands the highest price in Philadelphia market, and its quality depends on its genuine purity. Seeds should be two years old before sowing.

Rock Melon.—Fruit of an oval, round shape, rind green, with large white warts or rocky appearances thereon, hence its name. Flesh solid, of a yellowish color, rich and melting; in size, equal to the former.

CULTURE.—The Melon is cultivated in a similar manner to the Cucumber. The soil and treatment that grows the one will grow the other, though the Melon prefers a dryer atmosphere, and is more liable to die off after heavy rains than the former. To have it in perfection, it should not be grown in the vicinity of Squashes, Gourds, Pumpkins, Cucumbers, or any variety of the family, or it will invariably become impregnated with the inferior flavor of its congeners. In a small Garden, it is not possible to grow all these sorts without contamination. It is therefore better to plant all Squashes and Pumpkins in the field. A bed twenty-two feet square will grow sixteen hills, each six feet apart. Mark the spaces by the line each way; dig out the earth one foot deep and two feet wide, spreading it about; then fill up the holes thus made six inches higher than the surrounding ground, with rich, light compost—very old, rotten manure, sand, and garden earth, in equal parts, will do. Into these conical heaps or hills, about the first of May, sow eight or ten seeds, half an inch deep and a few inches apart. As soon as the plants have made two rough leaves, thin them out, leaving four only to each hill. When each have made four or five rough leaves, pinch the point of each shoot to make the plants branch out and fruit earlier; this is what gardeners call "topping," which strengthens the vines. Draw earth around their stems to support them from the wind; when they begin to run, they require no further assistance, except it may be to thin out the shoots where they become too crowded and confused. Hoe and stir up the soil, and keep clear of weeds. As no garden should have a foot square of lost ground, crop between these hills. Valentine, or Snap-Short Beans, is very suitable. Three sorts sown now will be off the ground in June and July, before the Melon vines occupy the whole. This plant, with the Cucumber, is very subject to be attacked with a yellow striped, or black bug. We are not yet aware of an infallible remedy, but a dusting of soot or wood ashes will retard their progress till the plants begin to grow freely. If they are thus attacked as soon as the vines show their rough leaves, it would be imprudent to top the plants, as it stops their growth, and the insect would then entirely overcome them.

Melons may be forced, in the same way as directed for the Cucumber, when it can be conveniently done, and to my taste it is a preferable plant; the finer sorts, that will not bear the open exposure of rain and heat, should be sown, such as the Green-fleshed and Rock Melons. Some of the latter, and as fine as any I ever saw, took the first premium at the New Jersey Horticultural Society, at Princeton, the past season. They were from the garden of A. H. Stevens, Esq., of Hoboken, and did great credit to the grower. When grown under glass, the sash should have a *very thin* mat thrown over it, from eleven to two o'clock, and from the middle of April till the fruit is all cut; and although the leaves may droop, it is not always a sign that the plant is in want of moisture. It is not advisable to pour the water round the neck of the plant—a very common practice and a very inconsistent one; the extremity of the roots and leaves are the absorbing organs of the plant; supply the former by watering the soil, and the latter by frequent sprinklings with the syringe, or from the rose of a watering pot.

The red spider is a pest to the Melon. It is a very minute red insect, quick in its movements, generally on the under side of the leaf. When observed, lift up the vines and turn them over, exposing the under surfaces of the leaves; then give them a syringing with soap suds. One or two such doses will destroy it, when pure water may be more frequently used, for it is too dry an atmosphere that genders this pest of the gardener.

Within a few years past, Europe has resounded with the praise of very extraordinary Melons from Persia and Cabul, so much so that we were induced to import two varieties to test their merits in this climate. One variety was very small, about half a pound weight, of a fine, smooth, round form, flesh quite yellow and high flavored, but too small for general culture. The other was opposite in every character, being large, oval, with a rough, white rind, flesh reddish-yellow, looked very tempting, but tasted much like a Pumpkin. Each seed cost sixpence sterling.

WATER-MELON.

Cucúrbita Citrúllus.—*Melon d'eau*, Fr.—*Wasser Melon*, Ger.

The Water Melon is purely a tropical fruit, wisely adapted to the wants of the inhabitants of those countries, who greatly appreciate it for its refreshing coolness, and delicious flavor. It is a grateful beverage in warm weather. It is no way nutricious, but its seeds are considered a valuable remedy in urinary complaints. There are several sorts cultivated extensively in New Jersey, even to thousands of acres, for the supply of the Philadelphia and New York markets, viz.:

Long Green, *Mountain Sprout*, *Carolina*, *Spanish*, and occasionally a White variety—all fine sorts, though we prefer the

Spanish. It is round, very dark green, having a very thin rind, with a bright red flesh, and black seeds. It does not grow so large as some others, but is more rich and sugary in flavor, and commands a better price. It was introduced to this country about eighteen years ago. The seed of the first that I saw, was brought from Portugal, by a supercargo of one of the ships of the late Henry Pratt, Esq., of Lemon Hill, who freely distributed the seeds to his friends.

CULTURE.—They require a light, sandy soil, not over rich. Plant them in hills as directed for Melons, giving them more room, as their vines extend much further. The seeds should be two years old before planting. If they are wanted of a large size, three or four fruit from each plant will be sufficient, and when one fruit only is taken, they will grow to from twenty to thirty pounds weight each. It will injure the flavor of the fruit if they are grown near to other varieties of the Melon.

MINT.

Mêntha Virìdis.—Menthe, Fr.—*Münze*, Ger.

THERE are several varieties of Mint, but the one under consideration is commonly known as Green Mint, or *Spear Mint*, from its long-pointed leaves. In its green state, it is used in sauces, salads, and frequently in soups. When dried, and taken as a tea, it is very efficacious in stomach complaints, far surpassing any alcoholic preparation.

CULTURE.—It is a perennial plant, and propagated by parting the roots in Spring. It will grow in any kind of soil where moisture abounds, and if in a sheltered spot, will come forward more early for use. If required to be cultivated extensively, draw drills two inches deep, and one foot apart, drop therein small pieces of the root, six inches apart; cover them with the soil; and give the ground a good top-dressing every year with manure, or rich earth. A bed will keep in bearing five or six years. When new plantations must be made, it is cut when the shoots are a few inches high. If the plants are wanted for drying, they must be allowed to grow till they are in full bloom, when they are to be cut, and the stalks laid out thinly to dry, in a shed or airy out-building. When they are perfectly dry, and have a brittle feeling, tie them up in a paper to keep till wanted. When green Mint is very desirable, it can be taken up and planted in boxes, and forced in a hot-bed with very little trouble. In two weeks the plants will be fit to cut. Two years ago, I was forcibly struck with the abuse of this very healthful herb. My physician prevailed upon me to pay a visit to one of the Springs, in the interior of this State, to try the effect of its waters upon my system, then greatly reduced by an accident. To me, every table appears meagre, unless it has a very liberal supply of good wholesome vegetables. On this occasion, the table of " mine host" appeared to have very homœopathic dishes of my favorites. When my strength began to recruit, I sallied forth to the garden to observe the cause, when behold it contained almost exclusively *Green Mint!* I could not conceive what extensive use they made of it, till on being more familiar with the establishment, I observed that it was carried in armsful (as if for feeding cattle) to the barroom, where it was liberally saturated with brandy, ice, and sugar, to foster an appetite for the sons of Bacchus. May that Boniface live to learn that Cabbage, Beans, and Peas, are better for health and happiness than mint-juleps!

MOREL.

Phállus esculéntus.—*Champignon*, Fr.—*Essbare*, Ger.

THIS vegetable is a native of this country, and closely related to the Mushroom, from which it is distinguished by the cap being hollow within, and adhering to the stem by its base, and latticed on the surface with irregular sinuations. The height is about four inches. It is in perfection, and will be found from May to September, in wet banks, in woods, and in moist pastures, and should not be gathered when wet with dew, or soon after rain; if gathered dry, they will keep several months. They are used either fresh or dried, as an ingredient to heighten the flavor of gravies, ragouts &c.

CULTURE.—We are not aware that this vegetable has been introduced into garden-culture, like the Mushroom, but there can be no doubt of the attempt being attended with success. The spawn should be collected in June, and planted into dung-beds, or ridges of soil differently composed, in order by experiment, to come to the best mode of cultivation. Those who have practised the growing of Mushrooms, will find no difficulty in cultivating the *Morel* or *Mascul* plant.

MUSHROOM.

Agaricus campèstris.—Champignon cultivè, Fr.—*Pitz*, Ger.

THE Mushroom has afforded a wide field of speculation for botanists and naturalists, who have disputed of its perfect or imperfect character—the peculiar method of its propagation and growth—and its close assimilation in taste to animal matter. The growth and formation of this humble plant is the most remarkable in the vegetable kingdom.

They are extensively used for making Catsup, esteemed as a pickle, and when stewed with rich gravies, are considered by some very delicious. They are extensively cultivated in Europe, particularly in Britain, where they are grown all the year round. They have also drawn the attention of the more scientific gardeners in this vicinity, within these few years past, and basketsful have been brought before the Pennsylvania Horticultural Society in our Winter and Spring exhibitions. The genuine Mushroom is found in Autumn, on rich, old pastures. It has a small, round, brownish-white head, of a delicate pink color underneath: the stem is generally from two to three inches high. There are frequent accounts of deaths caused by this vegetable, attributable either to excess in eating, or to a want of care in selecting the pure article, which grows invariably in open fields—such as are overtopped by trees, or growing in the shade, must be avoided; also those that grow rapidly, five or six inches high, bladder-like, or have a bright-red, fine-wrought net-work underneath, and of a disagreeable scent; those possessing such characters, are bad and even poisonous.

Mushroom Spawn.—We copy from the transactions of the London Horticultural Society, the following approved method of making Mushroom Spawn:

" In June or July, take any quantity of fresh horse-droppings (the higher fed the better) mixed with short litter, one-third of cow's dung, and a good portion of mould, of a loamy nature; cement them well together, and mash the whole into a compost. Spread it on the floor of an open shed, to remain till it becomes firm enough to be formed into square flat bricks; which done, set them on edge, and frequently turn them till half dry; then with a dibble make two or three holes in each brick, and insert in each hole a piece of good old spawn, about the size of a walnut," or the spawn which consists of fine white threads that may be found where mushrooms are growing in pastures. " The bricks should then be left till they are dry. This being completed, level the surface of a piece of ground, under cover, three feet wide, and of sufficient length to receive the bricks; on which lay a bottom of dry horse-dung, six inches thick; then form a pile, by placing the bricks in rows, one upon another, with the spawn side uppermost, till the pile is three feet high; next cover it with a small portion of warm horse dung, sufficient in quantity to diffuse a gentle glow of heat through the whole. When the spawn has spread itself through every part of the brick, the process is ended, and the bricks may then be laid up in a dry place for use." Mushroom Spawn, made according to this direction, will preserve its vegetative power many years, if well dried before it is laid up; but if moist, it will grow and exhaust itself.

Culture.—Of late years, the cultivation of this luxury has become so simplified, that it is in the power of every farmer and cottager to grow the article for use or sale. Any time in October or November, collect from the stable daily the fresh droppings, throw them into a heap, which prevent from heating violently, by frequent turnings, and spreading it out thinly, defending it from rain or water of any kind. When the quantity of one, two, or three loads (according to resources) has accumulated, and has lain in a heap two or three weeks, (which time it will most likely require for all the parts to get into an equal fermentation), as soon as it is observed that the fiery heat and rank steam of the dung are gone off, it is ready for use. Mushrooms can be grown in cellars, sheds, stables, or in any other such building, where they will be protected. Where it is intended to cultivate them permanently, a covered shed will be found the most convenient place in which to perform the necessary work. For this purpose a dry situation should be chosen, the more sheltered the better, on which to build a shed of sufficient dimensions. A bed four feet wide, and twelve feet long, will give an ample supply for a moderate-sized family. The shed may however be erected ten feet wide and sixteen feet long, giving space for working materials, and two beds if required. The shed should run from north to south, having a close roof, and weather-boarded. With the exception of four apertures as windows, to be covered with shutters, this erection might be made ornamental having a portion of it for a tool-house. Having marked out the space for the bed, throw out the earth about six inches deep, laying it regularly at the side, and if good, it will do for earthing the bed. In the trench, lay four inches of good dung, not too short, for forming the bottom of the bed; then lay on the prepared dung, about six inches thick, regularly over the surface, beating it down firmly with the back of the fork. Put on other six inches, and so on till eighteen or twenty-four inches thick. In that state it may remain ten or fifteen days, during which time the heat should be examined about the middle of the bed, by thrusting a small stick in several places, and when found of a very mild heat, the bed may be spawned. The spawn bricks for this purpose should be broken regularly into pieces about an inch and a half or two inches square. These pieces are best put in with the hand, raising the dung up a few inches with the one, while with the other the spawn can be laid in and covered. This ought to be done in every six inches of the surface of the bed. If the sides of the bed are made of a sloping form, they can also be spawned. After spawning, level the surface with the back of the spade, beating it gently, after which it may be earthed. Procure that of a sandy, loamy nature, if from a pasture, so much the better. Break it up and make it fine, laying it on two inches thick. Level it very neatly with the rake, and beat it closely and evenly. When the whole is finished, the bed must be covered, a foot thick, with good clean straw or natural hay, over which lay mats or canvas in severe weather. Examine the bed every few days, and if the heat increases, diminish the covering of straw, which is better than to take it off altogether. In about five weeks, if the bed be under proper cultivation, Mushrooms will make their appearance, and in two days more they will have grown to a sufficient size for use. Some people cut them, but it is decidedly better to give them a gentle twist in the ground and draw them out, filling up the cavity with a little fine mould, gently pressed in level with the bed. This method of gathering is much better than *cutting*, as the part left generally rots and breeds insects, particularly the wood-louse, which is very destructive to Mushroom beds.

Sometimes it happens that a bed suddenly ceases to be productive. This may arise from various causes, but most frequently from the cold state of the bed in Winter, or a dryness of soil. In the former case, an additional covering should be given, in the latter, water in a milk-warm or tepid state should be applied moderately, for two or three mornings in succession. After each watering leave the covering off for about an hour. Soft water should be used for the purpose. In Summer the beds will require watering every two days, though in Winter they may not need it in as many months. A good bed will be productive for three months, though it may occasionally happen to wear out in half that time.

From these observations, an ingenious mind can make a Mushroom bed in a multitude of situations, all obtainable where there are cellars, stables, or other buildings. We would not despair even in the open air during Winter, covered with plenty of litter, under a few boards to ward off cold rains. In Spring and Summer, any quantity may be grown in this way.

It will be observed, in the cultivation of every other vegetable we either sow or plant some evident material of reproduction; but in the cultivation of Mushrooms, we neither sow nor plant any antecedent production of seed, plant, or root, yet it is certain that mushrooms are reproduced by a process in which the dung of certain animals forms the chief instrument, and on the goodness and strength of that ingredient, in whatsoever way it is made, chiefly depends the crop. We are aware that this vegetable appears in certain situations without any apparent cause, though we feel fully satisfied that there are inert ingredients that only require a combination of influences to produce certain results, and these results in nature are unerring.

The young Horticulturist should never desist from making moderate and well-considered experiments. Let him never suppose that perfection has already been attained. Acumen and perseverance should be pre-eminently conspicuous in the gardener, who has many vicissitudes by weather, insects, and accidents to encounter, and he should be prepared with resources to resist them all.

MUSTARD.

Sinàpis álba et nìgra.—*Moutarde*, Fr.—*Senf*, Ger.

Mustard Seed was first obtained from Egypt, and has been known and cultivated for many hundreds of years. It is extensively used both in its natural state and manufactured, and is considered a wholesome condiment, in whatever way it is taken or prepared. It assists digestion, warms the stomach, and promotes appetite. In the Spring, in its green state, when mixed with salads, it is very refreshing, and ought to be extensively cultivated for that purpose. In Europe it is vastly appreciated, but with us little attention is given to the subject. There are two varieties. The *White* is principally used for garden purposes, and the seed used medicinally. We can speak practically of its beneficial effects in constipation of the bowels.

One or two table spoonsful a day, sipped from half a tumbler of water, and swallowed whole, is a great relief in dyspeptic cases, and many have been completely cured by its constant use. The London or Durham Table Mustard is made from this species. *Black* Mustard is of the same flavor, and considered of equal efficacy with the White. From the flour of this variety the American mustard is made.

Culture.—This salad is cultivated in the same manner as recommended for Cress, at all times of the year—sowing every week or two, either in beds or drills, or for early use in hot-beds or boxes, in the windows of a warm room. The seeds should be covered very slightly, and frequently watered, as moisture is indispensable to its growth. It should always be cut when about an inch high, using a sharp knife, and cutting close to the ground, holding the tops in one hand whilst the knife is used with the other. They should be carefully washed from earth or sand, allowing them to be as short time in the water as possible; neither should they be gathered long before using, for their flavor would be thereby impaired. As much of this seed is generally required, a portion should be sown very early to produce it. A bed three feet wide and twenty feet long, having the plants four or six inches apart, will produce a sufficiency of seed for every domestic purpose.

NEW ZEALAND SPINACH.

Tetragònia expánsa.—Epinard d'éte, Fr.

THE great advantage this Spinach possesses over the other varieties is that of supplying a crop of leaves in the dryest weather, when crops of other sorts have failed. From its rapidity of growth, a few dozen of plants will afford a supply during its growing season. If a few leaves of Sorrel are boiled with it, the flavor is improved.

CULTURE.—It is a spreading, towering plant. growing in a circular form, attaining the height of four or five feet. Sow the seed very thinly, in rows one inch deep and two feet apart, about the first week of April, in an open, rich piece of ground. Hoe freely and keep clean of weeds. The seeds, in a green state, make an excellent pickle, for which alone it is worth cultivation.

NASTURTIUM.—*See* INDIAN CRESS.

ONION.

A'llium cèpa.—Oignon, Fr.—*Zwbiel*, Ger.

THE Onion was anciently called *Cepe*, on account of the form of its bulb. It was also termed *Unio*, because the bulb never divided: hence the English name Onion is derived. It is supposed to be a native of Spain, though its native country and date of introduction is not certainly known. No vegetable is more extensively known and cultivated than the Onion. It has been the common seasoning for meats and soups of all nations, from the earliest period to the present—gracing the table of all classes of society, in some form or other. For flavoring, it is indispensable in cookery. Besides imparting its flavor to other preparations, it affords considerable nutriment, and is considered to possess medicinal properties of considerable value. However, when improperly taken, and in too great quantities, it loses its virtues and becomes unwholesome and indigestible. Used in its crude state, it often remains in the stomach forty-eight hours before being dissolved by the gastric juice, and in this state has been known to produce spasms. They are most agreeable, when boiled and served up with sauce or drawn butter. When cooked in this way, they are greatly improved by the water being changed when they are about half-boiled. Pour on the second water from a boiling kettle, throwing in a little salt. When Onions are used as stuffing, in combination with other substances, they should first be chopped very small and thrown into boiling water, and boiled for about five minutes; they should then be put into a colander to drain, and pressed till not a drop of water remains. If they are then mixed with the other ingredients, they can be eaten without any inconvenience or injury to the stomach. Roasted and fried Onions should be avoided by persons of weak digestive powers. There are a multitude of varieties in cultivation; but the most useful are the following

Strasburg, or Yellow Onion. Large oval, inclining to flat; very hardy, keeps well and of strong flavor.

Silver Skinned.—White, flat, medium size. Very generally used for pickling.

Red Dutch.—Dark red, medium size, inclining to flat, keeps well, very hardy, extensively grown in the Eastern states for export, strong flavor.

Portugal, very large, globular, mild flavor; does not keep well.

Potato, or under-ground Onion; produces a quantity of young bulbs on the parent root, which should be planted in rows, in March, three inches deep (below the surface) and six inches from bulb to bulb, eighteen inches being left between the rows. Keep them clear of weeds, and earth them up like potatoes, as they continue to grow. They will be fully grown about the first of August, when they may be treated as other Onions.

Welsh or *Tree Onion.*—Much grown in cold countries, where the Onion does not seed freely. This variety shoots up a stem on which small bulbs grow in place of seeds. These pea-bulbs are kept till next year, when they are planted and produce very good roots of considerable size, while the stem gives a farther supply for next year's planting. There are other varieties: such as *Globe*, *James's Keeping*, *Tripoli*, *Reading*, and *Deptford;* but none of them, for this climate, surpass or even equal those described.

Culture.—The soil in general cannot be too rich for this esteemed vegetable, and however good it may be, it requires more or less manure for every crop. It is a plant with a number of roots, that ramify to a great extent, absorbing nourishment from every particle of the soil. In regard to rotation of crops, the Onion is an anomalous case: for the same ground has been known to produce yearly, for nearly half a century, heavy crops. I have seen instances of twenty-two successive crops of Onions from the same ground, it having had every season a supply of cow, hog, or barn-fowl manure. There are hundreds of acres grown in this vicinity for shipping to the southern market. The system pursued is to manure the ground heavily, with the best of dung. Dig or plow the ground early in Spring; level it well with the rake or harrow; then with the Beet rake draw drills about one and a half inch deep and about nine inches apart, leaving a space of about fifteen inches between every three drills, called an alley. Plant these drills with young Onions, about the size of Beans, and do not cover them. They will be green in a few days. Hoe frequently and keep clear of weeds. In June, dig the alleys and plant them with late Drumhead Cabbage and Savoys for a Winter crop, or large York for a Fall crop. The Onions will be ripe in July, when they are pulled and cleared off. The soil must then be dug up and well broken, to allow the Cabbage crop to extend and grow freely. This is the system pursued by our market gardeners; but one error they all commit, and in consequence are not able to keep full-grown Onions over Winter, the bulbs rotting and decaying, from the drills having been drawn too deep, and pulling the crop two or three weeks too soon. My method is, after the ground has been well dug and raked even, to roll it before the drills are drawn, which must not exceed half an inch deep, being merely a mark whereon to lay the sets. Hoe to keep down the weeds; lift the crop after the tops are fully dried off; expose them in the sun a few days, to harden them; take them to a shed and spread them out thin, to dry; or tie them up in ropes and hang them up for use; by this treatment they will keep perfect throughout the whole Winter.

Sowing Seed.—The general method is to sow the seed very thickly, in shallow drills, early in April. The bulbs grow to the size of Peas or Beans by the middle of July, when they are lifted and put away in an airy loft, to keep till next Spring

They are then planted out in drills for a full crop, as above. *Onions* may be grown from the seed in one season, fully large enough for culinary purposes, and where the soil is of a deep mellow loam, on a dry bottom, which is most genial to the growth of this bulb, they will grow equally as fine as those that have taken two seasons to mature. For this purpose, sow the seed very thinly, (half an inch apart is thick enough, and an ounce of seed will be ample supply for a family)—in drills nine inches apart, and as shallow as they possibly can be drawn. Tread the seed in with the foot, to make it firm. Sprinkle a very small portion of fine earth over the seed, and finish by raking it evenly. Within three weeks the Onions will make their appearance, when, if many weeds rise among them, they must be cleared with a small hoe, observing not to hoe deep, for the more the Onion rises out of the ground, it is the finer, and keeps better. As soon as the plants are three inches high, thin them out to two inches apart. If the weather is moist, the thinnings may be transplanted into other ground. They too will attain a full size, but observe, in planting, to put the roots only under ground. The plants being now two inches apart, as they grow, every alternate one should be pulled for immediate use, either for soups or salads, leaving the crop four inches apart in the row. Nothing further will be required until they are pulled up for drying, except the keeping down of weeds, which must be strictly attended to.

In moist seasons, Onions are apt to grow (what is termed) thick-necked; in such cases they should, about the end of July, be gently bent down with the handle of the hoe, or the head of a wooden rake, which will check their rapid growth, and cause them to bulb sooner. About the middle of September, sow a row or two of Onion-seed for early Spring use, before any other green salading or seasoning can be obtained; the plants will be four inches high before Winter sets in severely, when they should have a little rough litter thrown over them. or a row of Spruce branches stuck among them for protection.

They will come very acceptably into use in March and April; or a few of the large Onions can be planted in September; they will divide into several roots or scallions, and can be drawn for use as above, and a few more can be planted early in Spring, to draw for the same purpose.

SEED SAVING.—It is very important to have good seed, therefore, select the most uniform roots in September, and plant them fully under ground, in rows one foot apart, and two feet from row to row. Let the ground be in excellent condition, for the stronger the plants, the finer the seed, which will be ripe in July or August, according to the weather. As soon as the heads begin to open and show the black seeds, they must be cut off and put into a sheet to dry. Clean it out well when perfectly dry—all seeds keep best in bags hanging in an airy room, and Onion seed will be perfectly good for three years. To grow Onions for *pickling*, sow the seed thinly in a bed in March or April, at the same time that the general crop is planted. No further culture is required, except hand-weeding, as their thickness in the bed will prevent their growing large, and will cause them to come to maturity sooner. They should be lifted in clear sunshine weather, as it improves their color. The White or Silver-skinned is the sort usually grown for this purpose.

The Onion crop is an interesting portion of gardening to every good housewife. She is ever solicitous that it should be full and certain. As it requires to be powerfully manured, we throw out the following hints for her special use. As we have intimated, Onions will grow on the same soil year after year, without any deterioration, provided it is liberally supplied with nutrition; for this purpose the following ingredients, always plentiful about every house, and generally thrown to waste, can be most beneficially applied. Soot spread over the ground, either before or after the crop, or thinly over the young plants—urine thrown over the ground during the Winter season—soap-suds, any time in the Fall or Winter, in like manner. These are not mere theoretic ideas; they are practical facts, which can be illustrated by any person who has the materials at command. I have seen Guano used to this crop, both with bad and beneficial results. At the rate of four hundred pounds to the acre, the Onions were greatly improved in size, though not in their keeping qualities. Applied at the rate of eight hundred pounds to the acre, the roots of the crop suffered, the plants got yellow, and did not fully recover their appearance. This manure should always be used in a liquid state, and about the strength of twenty-five pounds to a hogshead of water, to be applied after having stood twenty-four to forty-eight hours—urine can be used in the same manner, after being reduced with six parts of water. Every good householder who cultivates a garden, should have a large cask, in some retired corner, to form a deposit for the refuse of the wash-house. which can be reduced with a part of water, and applied to all vegetable crops in time of need; or where the soil is not rich enough, the plants can be fully watered with it, in the evening, once a week while they are in a growing state.

OKRA, OR OCHRO.

Hibíscus esculéntus.—*Gombo*, Fr.

This plant has been introduced to our notice and table from the West Indies, where it is cultivated to some extent as a vegetable. The green seed pods are put into soups, or stewed and served up with butter. It is becoming very popular with us, and grown to a great extent by some gardeners for supplying the market.

Culture.—The seeds are sown thinly, on dry, warm soil, in shallow drills two feet apart, about the same time as the Lima Bean Cover the seeds lightly. Sometimes they come up and are cut off with the frost; if so, plant again. An ounce of seed will supply any family. After the plants are up, thin them out to nine inches apart; hoe freely, and draw a little earth to the stems as they continue to grow. They will reach the height of five feet in good soil. The pods must be gathered when about an inch and a half long and quite green. As soon as they become brown and hard, they are useless for the kitchen.

PARSLEY.

A'pium Petroselinum.—Persil, Fr.—*Petersilie,* Ger.

The Garden Parsley is a biennial plant, a native of Sardinia, and is a very useful and pleasant vegetable; esteemed for many qualities besides that of garnishing. Its seasoning flavor, for soups and stews, is very agreeable to many. It also counteracts the smell of the breath after eating Onions. It may be preserved for seasoning, by drying it till crisp, in Summer; then rub it up fine between the hands, and put it away in a bottle for Winter use.

Culture.—The Curled variety only should be cultivated. It is more beautiful as a garnish than the plain, and requires very little more attention to keep it pure. Seed growers are not generally particular enough with this simple article; they ought, before the plants go to seed, to pull up all those that offer to be plain, reserving only those that are beautifully curled. Sow it in drills half an inch deep, early in April. These drills may form an edging round any compartments of vegetables, or along the walks. It will remain from four to six weeks before it vegetates, and, what is rather remarkable, seed four years old will vegetate sooner than seed of the preceding year. As soon as the plants get three or four inches high, thin them to six inches apart; cut down about a third part at a time, by which means a young stock will be kept constantly for use. Should any of the plain-leaved appear, root it out. An ounce of seed will suffice for any family.

To have fresh, green Parsley, at all seasons, should be the aim and ambition of every gardener, and it is rather a matter of surprise that our markets and tables are not more liberally supplied with this valuable Winter garniture. Keep it only from severe frost, and it will grow the whole Winter. For this object, select a warm spot of ground, light and rich, four feet by six; sow it early in the season; treat the plants as directed above; cut them all over in September, surround the bed early in November with boards, and cover with mats or shutters; if glass can be obtained, so much the better. By this process a sufficient supply in the severest weather will be always obtainable. If a frame and sash are out of reach, procure some branches of Spruce, Pine, or Cedar, and cover the bed during December, January, and February. It will grow tolerably well under such protection.

PARSNEP.

Pastinàca Satìva.—Panais, Fr.—*Pastinake,* Ger.

THE Parsnep is a biennial plant; that is, a plant that lives two years, seeds, and dies, like the Onion, Carrot, and Turnip. It is a native of Europe, and is a profitable and desirable root for family use in Winter and Spring, being both wholesome and nourishing, and should be cultivated abundantly in every kitchen Garden. Parsneps contain a considerable portion of sugar, and are more nourishing than either Carrots or Turnips. They make an excellent marmalade. Wine also, to some extent, is made from them. They are principally used at the table with boiled meats, though they make a very excellent dish after being boiled, sliced thinly, and dipped into a thin batter of flour and butter, or eggs, and afterwards fried brown. In my native country, Scotland, they are beaten up with potatoes and butter, and eaten with milk, making a very agreeable cottage dish. In an agricultural view they are valuable, for milch cows eat them with avidity, and yield an abundance of milk of rich and pleasant flavor, being preferable to the Carrot or Turnip for the purpose, which impart their taste to the milk. There are three varieties of the Parsnep, two only of which are desirable.

Guernsey Parsnep, an improved variety of the Common, grows large, and in deep light soils will attain the length of two feet.

Sugar, or *Hallow Crown.*—This is the best variety for Garden culture. It is of more uniform growth, has a smoother and cleaner tuber, and is equally as hardy and better flavored than the former, from which it is easily distinguished by the leaves arising from a cavity on the top, or crown of the root.

Culture.—Any soil suitable for Carrots will be found favorable for the Parsnep. Deep sandy loam is their delight. If it is not naturally so, it should be dug twenty inches deep, as directed for trenching, page 8. Sow any time from March to May, in drills, one inch deep and fourteen inches from drill to drill. Scatter the seeds thinly, and cover neatly and evenly with the rake. As the plants grow, thin them out occasionally and finally, till they stand eight inches apart in the row. In three weeks the seeds will appear, from which period till the leaves cover the ground, the soil must be stirred with the hoe every week or two. In October the leaves will begin to turn yellow, which is a certain sign of their maturity. They may then be dug up for use, as they are wanted. They will stand any severity of frost, so that it is necessary only to lift as many as will supply the family till the frost leaves the ground. They should be lifted their full length, and not cut with the spade, which injures them. Store away a sufficient supply for Winter use, in time of severe frost, leaving a balance in the ground for Spring supply, and some to go to seed. The seed keeps only two years—an ounce will supply a family.

PEA.

Pisum Sativum.—Pois, Fr.—*Erbse*, Ger.

THE Pea is of great antiquity as a culinary vegetable, and is familiar in the domestic cookery of every country. It is an annual, the seed being sown and matured in the same season, and in some varieties in an incredibly short space of time. They are considered a pleasant and nourishing food, having the character of purifying the blood and correcting scorbutic humors. In flavor and quality there is as great a difference in the Pea as in any vegetable with which I am acquainted, though, from observation, cultivators nd even cooks have little knowledge of the quality and flavor of the different varieties in cultivation. Some, when merely plain boiled and seasoned, are of themselves a luxury; others require more assistance from the culinary art to make them palatable. It is not our object to detail the various modes of cooking, yet we confess that we have seen them *mis-boiled.* The earlier sorts take from half an hour to three quarters; the Marrow-fats, from fifteen to twenty minutes, according to age. To have their flavor perfect, they should be picked, shelled, and cooked, all within three or four hours. When kept over night their quality is greatly impaired. Some prefer them boiled with a bunch of mint; t e only seasoning admitted by others, is a little salt in the water.

We will not detail the numerous sorts we grow or are acquainted with, but the following will be found most useful for market or family supply. They are those most noted for their quality, and are arranged in the order in which they come to maturity.

Prince Albert.—A dwarf grower, pods and pea small, four days earlier than any variety we have yet tried, good flavor.

Extra Early.—A very early Pea that has been cultivated in this vicinity about fifty years, and was exclusively, for a long period, in the possession of a Mr. Cooper, near Camden, N. J., who, I am informed, obtained the seed from a German emigrant. It is the sort most extensively cultivated for our market, and for that purpose is preferable to any other, the crop being nearly all ready at once, when the ground can be cleared for a crop of Beans, or late Tomatoes.

Early Grotto.—A very superior family early Pea, both in size and flavor; three or four days later than the former, and continues a much longer time in bearing.

Early May.—A fine early variety, good flavored, and very productive.

Early Frame.—A very celebrated Pea in Europe, where its hardiness makes it a general favorite. It is an abundant bearer and an excellent family Pea.

Early Charlton.—A very hardy early Pea, which comes in well as a secondary crop.

Bishop's Dwarf.—A very remarkable dwarf variety, requiring no stakes nor support of any kind, except the earth drawn to its stems. It is very prolific, but does not do to sow late, as it is subject to mildew. It can be sown in rows eighteen inches apart. Draw the earth more to one side of the plants than the other, which will lay them all in one position, from which the crop can be more conveniently gathered.

The above varieties, with the exception of Bishop's Dwarf, should be sown about three feet apart. Give them all stakes or rods, for the double purpose of protecting them from the wind and to support the vines. With stakes the crop can be more readily gathered, and the plants will mature every pod. A quart of early Peas will sow four drills, each thirty yards long.

Royal Dwarf.—This succeeds the early varieties. It grows between three and four feet high.

B.ue Marrow.—A fine large Pea, very prolific and well fla vored, sown about first of May, will be fit for the table abou the fourth of July.

White Marrow.—Very generally cultivated, but is far sur passed by the

Matchless Marrow, being larger, equally as productive, and superior in flavor; grows five feet high.

Woodford Marrow.—A very green Pea, and boils without losing color. It makes the most beautiful dish of *green Peas*, and is an excellent bearer.

Surprise, if sown about the twentieth of March, will be fit for the table about the twelfth of June. A very excellent late Pea, of large size, and superior flavor.

Sugar Pea.—So called from its flavor. It is usually boiled in the pods whole, only drawing the thread from the back of the pod before it is put into the water. It can also be cooked in the usual way: a very sweet Pea; grows five feet high.

Knight's Dwarf Marrow.—This is called Dwarf, though it grows five feet, and should be sown in drills at least that distance apart.

Knight's Wrinkled Marrow.—There are several varieties of this, all of first-rate excellence. Though the ripe seed are peculiarly wrinkled and very untempting, yet the green fruit are exceedingly fine flavored.

Scimitar.—A large Pea and abundant bearer; takes its name from the shape of the pods; it is well flavored. Sown about the first of May; it will be ready about the sixth of July.

New Mammoth.—A very tall-growing Pea, requiring rods six feet high; a great bearer, of large size, and perhaps the very best flavored Pea grown. The only objection to it, is the quantity of ground it occupies. They should be planted two inches apart in the drills, and six feet from row to row. A quart will plant three rows, each thirty yards long. If sown about the first of May, it will be ready about the 12th of July

British Queen.—A wrinkled marrow Pea, of large size, and luscious flavor, grows five to six feet high; a new Pea of great excellence.

There are twenty or twenty-five other varieties of the Pea, but to go into a detail would be merely repeating what we have already said. They are generally mere varieties of those given, and so closely assimilated, that a name constitutes in most instances the only difference. The above list embraces varieties that become fit for the table in from six to ten weeks; and by repeated sowings, judiciously made, the garden will be supplied with Peas from May to frost. We believe that there is no vegetable in the catalogue so universally agreeable as the Pea. We have never heard any one say they could not eat well-cooked green Peas, and it should be an emulation to have them always at least in their season.

Culture.—The soil in which an early crop of Peas is sown, should be light, dry, and well sheltered. I have had great success with early Peas, by sowing a row along the south or east side of a board fence. This is done as soon as the frost is out of the ground—in some seasons about the first of March, while in others as late as the 19th. Such was the Spring of 1846, yet I had Peas fit for the table on the 17th of May. This is no criterion of the earliness of the Pea, for in 1844 I sowed Peas on the 30th of April, which were fit for the table on the 10th of June, being within six weeks, and on heavy, loamy soil. Ground for Peas should be well manured the previous year; if it is heavily manured for the crop, it causes them to grow more to straw than seed. As soon as they are two inches high, draw earth to them, and when they have grown a few inches more, repeat it again. When they are eight or ten inches high, this earthing greatly protects the vines, and keeps the wind from driving them about. After the final earthing has been completed, stake them. The stakes, or branches more properly, should be of a fan-form, and put in the ground in a slanting direction. On the other side of the row reverse the position of the stakes, which affords the vines more protection and security. When they show their first blossoms, it is a good plan to top off the point of the vine It then ceases to grow, and throws all its strength into the pods, by which they swell off more readily. Early Peas should be sown in drills two inches deep, and the seeds about one inch apart in the drills and two and a half feet from drill to drill. If stakes are scarce, two rows of Peas can be sown six inches apart, and then two rows the same way, four feet between each pair of rows. This is the general system, though I do not see what are its advantages. If the same quantity of seed be put into one row, it appears evident the product will be the same; but I have not satisfactorily tried the experiment. The height to which Peas grow very much depends upon the season and soil. Early sorts, in a dry Spring, will grow two feet, while in a moist season they will grow four. Many of the Marrow Peas in some seasons will grow six feet, and in others ten. The spaces between the rows of early Peas can be planted with Lettuce or Beans. The late kinds, where the rows are four to six feet apart, can be planted with early Celery—the vines will partially shade the young plants till they have taken root. The late Peas can also go on ground whence early Lettuce or Spinach has been taken. If the kinds we have named be sown from early in Spring to the 10th of May, a crop of young Peas will be in constant succession from May to the end of July. August, and the two first weeks of September, in this vicinity and South, will be in want of green Peas, which is very liberally supplied with the varieties of Beans. Early Peas may again be sown about the 15th of August. If the weather be dry, soak the Peas twenty-four hours in water before sowing. Indeed this is an excellent practice with all the tribe. When the ground is dry, the drills should have water poured into them before being planted, the seed will then grow at once, and not be in the least retarded, should the season continue dry. It will greatly prevent mildew if the Peas are watered in continued droughts.

The following mode of staking the tall varieties of the Pea is both cheap and simple, and possesses many advantages. Procure a number of stakes, in length according to the height of the Peas, and drive them into the ground on each side of the row, at the distance of six feet; pass a small line of cotton, or Onion-twine, along the poles, taking a turn on each. As the Peas advance, raise the next line higher, and so on, till they have attained their full height. Two lines will be enough, as the one line can be raised over the other. The air can circulate better through the vines than by the common method of staking.

Peas can be successfully cultivated by artificial means, and a good crop produced either in pits or very gentle hot-beds. For this purpose Bishop's Early Dwarf is most suitable. Sow in pots or boxes, rather thickly, and place them close to the glass till they are sufficiently strong for transplanting, when they may be carefully taken out, with the roots as entire as possible, and planted in frames or pits, from front to back, in rows fifteen inches apart, and two inches from plant to plant. Give plenty of air by day, should the weather admit of it, but keep them well covered at night. It may be observed, that in whatever way Peas are raised for forcing, they should invariably be transplanted. The temperature should be from 40° to 60°. When they appear dry, moderate waterings will be necessary, more especially in time of bloom, and when the pods are setting and swelling. Those who pay some attention to the cultivation of this very luscious vegetable, can very readily have them on the table from May to November in all ordinary seasons.

PEPPER.

Capsicum Annum.—*Piment,* Fr.—*Spanischer Pfeffer,* Ger.

THERE are several varieties of the Pepper cultivated for pickling and kitchen purposes—its natural locality is very generally diffused over all tropical countries, requiring in artificial culture a very warm locality, rich light soil, and careful cultivation. The green pods or small berries of all the varieties are used for pickling; the ripe fruit is dried and used in small portions as a seasoning of the hottest quality.

Bell, or Sweet.—Large bell-shaped and most esteemed for pickles, the skin being thick and more pulpy than any of the others.

Tomato, or Flat.—About the size and shape of the Tomato, is also very generally used for the same purpose; it is of a hotter nature than the former.

Cayenne.—Fruit small, round, tapering, long, or curved, and of the very hottest quality. We have seen about twenty varieties of the Pepper; their fruit, when ripe, from about the size of Peas to the size of Melons, and all of a bright red or bright yellow color.

CULTURE.—Sow a small portion of seed, thinly, half an inch deep, on a hot-bed or in a pot in a warm window, any time in March or April and transplant in May or June, on good ground, one foot apart, and eighteen inches from row to row. In a mild climate, sow at the same period in the open ground, in a small bed of light soil, and transplant when three to four inches high during moist weather, or water freely in time of planting. As they grow, hoe frequently, and earth up the stems similar to Cabbage.

POTATO.

Solānum tuberōsum.—Pomme de Terre, Fr.—*Kartoffel*, Ger.

THIS universal vegetable is a perennial, well known upon every table. It is a native of South America. In the vicinity of Quito, they are known under the name of *Papas*. They appear to have been known in Virginia as early as 1584, and were at that period cultivated by the Colonists. It is very amusing to observe the remarks of early writers upon their character, some saying they are only fit for "swine," while others recommend them as a delicate dish. It is a species of a very extensive family of plants, inhabitants of every part of the globe, all of a forbidding aspect, and not a few of them of the most deadly poison, while others are being extensively cultivated both as food and luxury to man. Among them are the Egg-plant and the Tomato. We are now arrived at a period of the history of the Potato when there appears to be a universal scourge or blight passed over the crop, in every country where it is cultivated—universal in its effects and as universally unaccounted for, some attributing it to one cause, while others take an altogether opposite view. It has always and does still appear to me to be an atmospheric disease, a kind of Cholera, as I termed it two years ago, which has threatened the past year nearly to extirpate the whole crop. We now predict that it has come to its height, and another season will produce a more healthy crop. Cultivation may promote health, though it will not avert the calamity. New soil in the past year has been more genial to the production of sound tubers, than old cultivated fields, though the former has not been entirely exempt from disease. The vines have always been affected after a few dull, cloudy, moist, warm days; these, succeeded by strong sunshine, made visible the first blighting effects. To cut off the stems close to the ground, as soon as the disease appeared, has invariably benfited, and in many instances, entirely saved the tubers, and we still hope that this root, which has been for many years a luxury to the rich and bread to the poor, will yet continue to improve, as it has done during the past hundred years. On the quality of the Potato, as used for food, a few words will suffice. It is the most nutritious of vegetables, where it agrees with the constitution, which is almost invariably the case, excepting some few instances where there is a spare or thin habit of body. To those who take much exercise in the open air, it is excellent food, and yields a very considerable amount of nourishment.

Too little attention is generally paid to the dressing of it; for an indifferent potato becomes good when well cooked, and a superior one gains every attraction that an appetite can desire.

An untinned iron saucepan is preferable to any other for boiling potatoes. In preparing them, they should never be peeled, or much of their nutritious quality is lost. They only require to be washed clean, and at farthest to be slightly scraped. After soaking in water for an hour, put them into the saucepan, with cold water sufficient to cover them; when it begins to boil, let a cupful of cold water be put in, which will check the boiling, and allow time for the potatoes to be done through, without their being in any danger of breaking When they are sufficiently soft, which may be known by trying them with a fork, pour off the water, and let the pot with the potatoes continue for a short time over a gentle fire, and the heat will cause any remaining moisture to evaporate; when, after being peeled, they will be fit for the table. By this method of cooking, if strictly adhered to, they will be found more palatable than under any other.

Various States and places have their favorite sorts. To enter into a general detail of their merits, would only produce conflicting opinions, for we are certain that what may do well in one State or country would fail in another. Mercer and Foxite for Pennsylvania, Pink-eyes and Mercer for New-York

Winnebagoes and Blue Jackets, for more eastern countries; but in no part of this country do we find the English, Irish, or Scotch Potatoes to succeed. We must look to our own exertions and industry in raising sorts from seed. If we wish to excel in quality, there is a very extensive field for improvement, and one that we can easily operate upon every year.

The Mercer, in this vicinity, is the universal favorite. The genuine sort is of a longish, flat, kidney form, with a liberal quantity of eyes, and pink-colored on the tapering end. Those covered with knotty protuberances are not considered so pure as those of a uniform shape. It is very early, a good bearer, and a good keeper.

Fox's Seedling, for garden culture and earliness, will be found preferable to the former. It is a round, white Potato, of good size and excellent flavor, when eaten from the ground, but will not retain its superior qualities for Winter use.

Foxite.—A yellowish-white Potato, with the eyes much sunk. It is a great favorite in some situations and soils, as a late variety. It is an excellent keeper, and well flavored.

No vegetable varies more in quality in different soils than this; for a sort that will be pleasant and well-flavored in one soil, will be coarse and rank in another. One fact may be observed, that white Potatoes do best on light soils, while red will be most productive on clayey or retentive soils.

Culture.—The first matter to be considered is the soil, which, if of a sandy loam, is better calculated for the potato than a heavy or very clayey soil. Though any soil will do, it must be observed that the roots produced in a light, are more dry and sweeter than those grown in a heavy soil. The finest potatoes are grown in a new, light, rich loam. If the soil is heavy, the manure used should be composed of well-decayed leaves, horse manure, and ashes, well blended and mixed together before using. A good crop can seldom be raised if this article is sparingly laid on. Two or three inches thick is a good manuring, but if that quantity cannot be obtained to cover the whole ground, put it three or four inches thick in the drill only whereon the sets are laid. It is not our purpose to enter into a labored dissertation on the culture of this esculent on a large scale, or we could easily show that it is but very imperfectly understood. Our object at present is garden culture, and our remarks are intended to apply to that branch. A gardener or farmer must be very low in the scale of his profession, unless he knows what crop is to follow another; and it is a point very necessary with potatoes that the ground be roughly dug before Winter, to have the soil well ameliorated before planting. Presuming that the ground is clear where the late Cabbage crop was taken from, dig it deeply and turn it up roughly for the action of the Winter; then, early in Spring, lay on your manure, and as soon as the ground can be worked, open a furrow the full depth of the spade. Lay therein three or four inches of dung, on which plant the sets with the eye upward, ten inches apart, eighteen to twenty inches from row to row. Dig over the ground and plant as you proceed. Sets for planting should be cut at least one week before planting, and spread out thin on a floor to dry. Potatoes of medium size can make from four to six sets. There is a great difference of opinion in regard to the size of the potato to be used for the purpose of planting, some carefully selecting the largest, others preferring the medium, and some retaining the smallest. We never put any regard upon the size of the tuber, though we are careful in observing the size of the set. In the event of their being small, we do not cut them; if of medium size, we make four to six sets; and if large, eight sets may be made. Again, the point of the potato is considered more early than the root-end, and some only use those eyes that are in the middle. We have never deemed this advantage worth much attention, though for a few very early planting we give preference to those eyes nearest the point of the tuber. As soon as they appear above ground, give frequent and deep hoeings, drawing earth carefully to the stems as they advance in growth. We assuredly detest the appearance of a weed among this crop, and frequently mourn and almost weep over fields of the rankest weeds where the undergrowth is potatoes. What can be expected from such slovenly husbandry—gardening we will not call it. The crop is thereby injured in quality and quantity, and not only that, but frequently disease ensues, which is attributed to the Potato *degenerating*. What an idea! Degenerate! no, never! All seeds, not only of this vegetable, but of every other, should be changed every three years at farthest; and we would change the kind of soil, or the Potato for seed, every two years. A change from light soil to heavy, or the reverse, will tend to benefit the quality, and if this cannot be effected, change with some of your distant friends, or make purchase from other States. We have said that early Potatoes should be planted as soon as the ground can be worked, which is from the 1st to the 20th of March. A few may then be planted in a very sheltered place, where they would not be much exposed to late frosts. The main crop should be planted about the 15th to the end of April. If left till a later period, they are very liable to be affected by the droughts of Summer, and take on an Autumn growth, which invariably injures the quality of the tuber. The maturity of the crop is readily known by the whitening of the stems, though they are fit for the table before that period. As soon as they are what is termed half-grown, a few may be lifted for use. Those intended for seed are considered better adapted for the purpose if they are not perfectly ripe, yet I doubt if this opinion is confirmed by experience. Writers on this subject too frequently reiterate the expressions of their predecessors. This is very observable among writers on horticultural and agricultural subjects. The experience of Abercrombie, Speechly and Knight is retailed as new matter for the present age, (advanced in every other science,) and is admitted as being as undeniable as any rule of Euclid. When passing through Ireland, that hot-bed of Potatoes, we observed them transplanting the stems that had grown six or eight inches from one part of the field to another, in the same way that Cabbages are planted, and I was informed the crop from those were fully as good as from the sets planted early in the season. This operation can be performed in a country where there is a great deal of moisture, or during very cloudy, moist weather, but in dry arid temperatures it would be a doubtful practice.

Artificial Culture.—Various are the methods by which Potatoes are forced, such as in frames, pits, hot-beds, under glass, or under shutters and mats. Whichever of these conveniences may be at hand, let there be from twenty inches to two feet of good manure in the bottom, over which place eighteen inches of good soil. Plant thereon your sets of Fox's Seedling, and cover them with four inches of earth. It is necessary that when finished the materials should be within six or eight inches of the glass. Sow over all some Early Short-top Scarlet Radish, which will be off before the Potatoes can be affected by their growth. To prevent their becoming long and spindling, give air on every favorable occasion, when there is sunshine, from ten to three o'clock, protecting them carefully at night. A few Lettuce may also be planted between the rows. They can be cut off as soon as they are in the way. This is making the most of every inch of ground, and every industrious gardener knows the value of time and space.

New Sorts from Seed.—We can never have Potatoes entirely suitable to our climate till we obtain such from seed—an operation rarely if ever attended to properly. For these experiments the field is very large, and certain to be crowned with successful results. A single *apple*, as they are called, collected in September or October, will produce two dozen new kinds; and if even half a peck of apples were collected, separate and wash the seeds from the pulp, dry them, and wrap them up in strong paper till Spring: about the middle of April, prepare a bed of fine earth, draw shallow drills thereon six inches apart and a quarter of an inch deep; sow the seeds thinly, and cover lightly with very fine earth. They will come up in two or three weeks. When they are two inches high, thin out a portion, lifting them very carefully with a trowel, and transplant them into a piece of well prepared ground, four inches apart and eight inches from row to row. Choose a moist, cloudy day for the purpose, hoe them freely, and earth them up a few times during the season. Treat the bed in like manner. In October, the roots will furnish a supply of small Potatoes, which must be taken up and a portion of the best preserved in sand during Winter, to be planted next Spring in the usual way. After they have had the ensuing Summer's growth, in October their tubers will have attained a sufficient size to determine their properties. It will be necessary to consider, not only the flavor of each variety, but the size, shape, color and fertility; also the earliness or lateness, rejecting all that have not every quality combined, for only such are worthy of permanent culture. It will thus be seen that with very little care and a little labor, new varieties may be produced and proven in the short space of two or three years.

Potatoes intended for keeping should be fully ripened before being taken up. When going through the process of lifting, drying, and storing, they should be handled with care, not filled up and emptied down as if they were as many stones. After having gone through this *stone-casting* process, nearly every Potato shows its effects when brought to the table, being covered with bruised marks in proportion to their rough treatment; whereas, if they are managed properly, every tuber would be as sound as on the day of its removal. Dry cellars, free from frost, are the most appropriate places of storage, and if they have a covering of sand they will not lose a particle of their flavor. If sand or dry earth is not used, give them a covering of straw, to prevent the air from giving the outside Potatoes an acrid taste. Towards the end of January and February, they should have a regular turning, to prevent their sprouting. If any have begun to grow, pick off the growths. They will require this operation repeated every few weeks while they are in the cellar. If this is not carefully attended to, and the Potatoes allowed to grow to any extent, they will lose much of their farinaceous quality. It is also very essential to turn over frequently those intended for seed, to prevent a premature growth. The greater the vegetative power of the set, the finer and stronger will they grow.

PUMPKIN, OR POMPION.

Cucúrbita, var.—*Courge*, Fr.—*Kürbis*, Ger.

We cannot think of admitting this vegetable into the precincts of a garden where there are Melons, Cucumbers, and other kindred plants. It would mix with and contaminate the quality of the more valuable sorts. If, however, there is an opportunity to plant a few in the field, among the Corn, we would recommend among the many sorts, the *Cashaw*, as being the best. There is a variety of a very coarse nature cultivated in the field, called the *Mammoth*, which frequently attains the enormous weight of two hundred and fifty pounds, and is only fit for pigs or cattle.

RADISH.

Ráphanus Satìvus.—*Rave*, Fr.—*Rettig*, Ger.

The native country of this well-known salad plant is supposed to be China. It is valued by us for its agreeable pur gency and grateful relish when mixed with salads, or eaten raw with bread and butter. They are supposed to possess medicinal qualities, abounding with a penetrating, nitrous juice, rendering them a good antiscorbutic. It is not admitted that they contain much nourishment. They should, however, when eaten, be very brisk and sprightly, always young; not tough, thready, nor overgrown. The young leaves make an agreeable mixture with Lettuce, Mustard, &c., as a green salad. There is an immense quantity of this article consumed in the Spring and early Summer season. It is a never-ending crop. Being of a rapid growth, it is up and consumed before the crops of Beets, Carrots, &c., make any headway, so that it occupies no ground as a crop by itself. There are many varieties, among which we select the following as most desirable.

Scarlet Short-top.—This is a long, tapering Radish, of a good scarlet color, with very short leaves. It is preferred by all gardeners, as it requires much less room than those with large tops, and is also the very earliest variety, when obtained pure.

Early Salmon.—Very similar to the former, though not of so bright a color, and is a few days later. It succeeds it very conveniently, and is of the same shape.

Olive-shaped.—This variety appears to be between the Scarlet Short-top and the Red Turnip Radish, partaking of both shapes (being a long oval) and maturing for the table between those two varieties.

White Turnip-rooted.—Very appropriately named, and highly esteemed. It succeeds those already described in maturing, and will bear the heat better, without becoming hard and stringy.

Red Turnip-rooted.—In shape and size like the White, matures at the same time, and when grown with it, makes a beautiful variety on the table.

Long White Portugal.—A very beautiful variety, in the shape of the Early Short-top. It does not come so soon as that sort, but makes a decided contrast with it.

White Summer.—A large, long, oval variety; cultivated for early Summer use, is of an excellent, mild flavor, bears the heat well, and is a beautiful variety.

Yellow Summer, or *Yellow Turnip-rooted.*—The very best for cultivating, and indeed the only one that stands the heat and drought with impunity. It is about an inch and a half or two inches in diameter, and from two to three inches long.

Black Spanish.—This is a Winter Radish, of very large size; Turnip form. It should be sown in August and September, lifted in October or November, and stored away in sand in the cellar for supplying the table in Winter. It will keep good till the following April.

Culture.—There are few vegetables that require less artificial care and culture than the Radish. For the Spring crop, it likes a light, rich, dry, sandy loam; but for later crops, a deep, moist soil is preferred. The first sowing should be made on a south or east border, with the Early Turnip-Rooted Beets. The Radish seed may be sown in drills between the latter, very thinly, covering them with about a quarter of an inch of fine earth. If the nights prove frosty, cover the border with straw, which will greatly advance the crop, and prevent its destruction. If sown about the first of March, and good weather ensue, they will be ready in the first week of April. A second sowing with some other crop, such as Carrots, should be made about two weeks later, and at the same time sow the Turnip-Rooted varieties. Another sowing, of all the Salmon and Turnip kinds, about the middle of April, to be followed with two sowings of White and Yellow Summer Radishes, at intervals, will be the principal crops for the season. Towards the end of August and September, Early Scarlet Short-top may again be sown; also the Black Spanish, as formerly directed. Should they be too thick, at any time, when fairly up, they must be thinned to an inch apart; for if allowed to grow crowded together; they will not produce a crop. It will take six or eight ounces of Radish seed to supply a family fully the whole season, though some writers amuse us by saying an ounce or two is enough. They must never have sown an ounce of Radish seed and seen its produce. If the weather is dry, at any of the sowings, the seed should have a few waterings, till it is fairly above ground; and even when they are growing, it is of much service in rendering the roots more crisp and better flavored.

Forcing Radishes.—Very little artificial heat is required to grow them in perfection. Make a gentle hot-bed about eighteen inches thick, on which place a frame. Fill in one foot of good, light, rich soil. After it remains a few days, to get warm throughout, sow the seeds rather thickly. Spread a small portion of fine soil over them; give the whole a gentle press with the back of the spade; put on the sash, and keep close till the seeds appear above ground; then air freely. If the plants are thick, thin them out at once to about an inch apart; water occasionally when the soil appears to get dry. If sashes are not to be obtained, shutters and mats make a tolerable substitute, and after the first of March, will do perfectly, though forcing early crops cannot succeed without the use of good glass sash. The best variety of Radish for the purpose is the Long Scarlet Early Short-top, or a variety of it called *Early Frame.* We have already alluded to the practice of sowing Radishes among the Cauliflower and Winter Lettuce.

Radishes sown for Seed should be kept apart from any other variety. If they are within three hundred yards of each other, they will mix. Where the Early Scarlet is wished very pure, it is our practice to transplant a few thousand every season to seed for early forcing. If it cannot be kept so far apart, save the seeds of two kinds every year, for three years; you will then have six sorts in culture, and the seed will keep three years perfectly. if in a dry place.

RHUBARB.

Rhèum rhapônticum.—*Rubarbe*, Fr.—*Rubarber*, Ger.

The Rhubarb of commerce is the root of the plant, which is principally grown in Asia, where it is dried and prepared for exportation to a very great extent. It is chiefly purchased by the Turks, who monopolize the trade as much as possible, and from it derive a large profit. It has been for centuries held in the highest estimation for its medicinal properties. It is a mild cathartic, and commonly considered one of the safest and most innocent substances of the class, though I have found that very large doses act as a very severe emetic; with its purgative virtues, it has a mild astringent one, and is found to strengthen the tone of the stomach. In addition to these qualities of the root, the stalk is allowed by all medical men to make one of the most cooling, wholesome, and delicious tarts that can be sent to the table; and though it does, at first, appear to some to have a peculiar flavor, yet they who use it very soon prefer it to any other fruit. Its rank flavor, however, entirely depends upon the age of the stalks; when young, they are entirely free from it. The varieties of Rhubarb for cooking forms an object of much interest and even great profit to the market gardener, and to every householder who has a garden it cannot be too highly recommended as a very salubrious vegetable for the family, either stewed or in tarts and pies. For dysentery in children it is an infallible remedy, stewed, seasoned with sugar, and eaten in any quantity with bread. The stalk is fit for use when the leaf begins to expand. Take the outside skin off the stalk, cut it into pieces about an inch long, put them into a saucepan and cover them with plenty of brown sugar and a few table-spoonsful of cold water; cover it, and let it stew slowly till perfectly soft; after having cooled, it is ready for use. Few vegetables have made a more rapid progress in their cultivation, within the past fifteen years, than this article, and we yet expect to see it cultivated by the hundred acres and brought to our market in wagon loads. The following sorts are all deserving of particular attention.

Tobolsk.—A very early, small, red variety, of excellent flavor for an early crop or forcing. It grows in very rich ground to about eighteen inches or two feet long.

Washington.—A green variety, very much spotted on the footstalks, grows two feet long, and is a second early sort.

Giant.—A very large green variety, with round stalks, that will grow four feet long, and nearly the thickness of a man's wrist. It is cultivated in England to an immense extent, as a late variety, to supply the market the whole Summer.

Mammoth.—This sort was raised by me from the seed of the former. It grows from three to four feet long, with stalks of great thickness, of a flat shape. It has taken the prize as the best Rhubarb, at the Pennsylvania Horticultural Society's meetings, the past three years. It is of excellent flavor.

Myatt's Victoria.—This is a red variety, of great excellence and richly flavored, grows very strong, equal to the Giant, and much earlier than that variety; is richly deserving of extensive culture.

Large Early Red.—A seedling, by me, from the Victoria. It is even larger than its parent, comes full eight days earlier, and will prove the best Early Rhubarb we have yet had brought to our notice. The stalks are three feet long, and are quite fit for use before the leaf begins to expand. It is richly flavored. It may be observed that the red stalked sorts are generally earlier than those with green stems.

Rheum palmatum, or Palmated-leaved Rhubarb, is the variety that is cultivated in China and Tartary for its roots, and in some countries another species, the *Undulatum*, is grown for the same purpose. There is no doubt that all the other varieties possess the same medicinal properties when they attain sufficient age, which is allowed to be seven years.

Culture.—Rhubarb is propagated either by seeds or by division of the roots. Where a great quantity is wanted the former process will have to be resorted to. Though the plants raised in this manner will not be of a uniform character, yet from seeds of the best kinds all will be worth cultivation. The seed should be sown as early as can be done in Spring. On light, dry soil, draw drills about an inch deep and one foot apart, in which sow the seeds thinly, and cover evenly. They will be up in about four weeks, and if the weather proves dry, give them occasional waterings. Hoe them freely to keep under the weeds. Sow a very few Radish seeds with them, and you will thereby see clearly where to use the hoe, and the Radishes will be pulled before the Rhubarb plants have made much progress. When they are an inch high, thin them out to four inches apart, and allow them to grow till October; at which time a piece of deep, rich ground should be selected, and dug eighteen inches deep, manuring it well with very rotten dung, and breaking and working it perfectly with the spade. When it has settled for about two weeks, set out the plants two feet apart in the row, and four feet between the rows. Plant their crowns two inches below the surface, and cover them four or five inches thick with leaves, or litter from the stable, to prevent the frost from throwing them out of the ground during Winter. No farther after-culture is required beyond keeping the ground clear of weeds. In the first year a crop of Lettuce, Beans, or Early Cabbage can be taken from between the rows, as the plants will not attain their full size for two years. In the early part of Winter, every year, cover the ground with a few inches of manure, digging it in with a fork, in Spring, among the roots. Rhubarb, thus treated, will continue many years in great perfection, and produce a very ample return. Where there are only a few roots wanted, they may be procured by the division of one or two good roots, leaving an eye to each, and planting them at once in ground prepared as above, where they are to remain About eight or ten plants will suffice for a small family, though twenty will not be too many. By this method it will be ready for use in the first year after planting, whereas, from seed, it is three years before it is ready for the table. In removing the stalks for use, first scrape away a little of the earth, then bend down the stalk you wish to remove, and slip it off from the crown without breaking or cutting it. The stalks should not be used after the leaves are full grown, as they are then too hard and stringy; use the stalks only of such leaves as are about half, or nearly fully expanded. Where there is a large supply, it can be made into a preserve of any kind. Both an excellent jam and jelly can be made from either the green or red varieties, though the color of that made from the latter is more beautiful, being a fine dark pink.

Artificial Culture.—To force Rhubarb, it is only necessary to procure some large pots, boxes, or half-barrels, and invert them over the roots. Then cover the whole entirely, ground and all, with leaves and hot stable-manure. This will cause an agreeable heat to arise; the plants will grow freely under their warm, dark covering; the stalks will be finely blanched, very tender, and delicately flavored. This operation should be performed before the ground gets frozen, by placing the boxes, &c., over the plants intended to be forced, and covering the ground with eight or ten inches of leaves or litter. Then, about the middle of January, mix with the leaves as many more, with warm dung, as will entirely cover the articles under which the plants are preserved. If properly managed, the stalks will be fit for use in from four to six weeks, and the plants will continue to produce till the roots in the open air take their place. They, too, are greatly benefited by placing a barrel over them as soon as they begin to grow in the Spring; the stems grow more tender and much longer by this process. There should be a few holes in the barrel, or a part of the bottom taken out to admit a little air, though it is not absolutely essential. Many persons may dislike all this trouble, and others have not the material at command; to such, we say, cover the roots with six or eight inches of any dry material, which will forward them two weeks before those that are uncovered. Others may have the convenience of a green-house under the stage, or some other warm building—even a warm closet, or a furnace in the cellar. In such situations the plants can be forwarded by planting them in November into large pots or boxes, with good earth, and placing them at any required time into any of these situations, giving water freely when they begin to grow. A crop will be obtained in a space of time varying according to the heat that is at command. After the plants have done producing stalks for culinary use, they may be turned out into a half shady, rich piece of ground, in May, when, after a season's growth, they can again be used for the same purpose. Hotbeds, frames or pits, will also do for forcing this article; but in such a case, the glass must be darkened to cause them to grow and blanch. The atmosphere must also be freely saturated with water, to make the stalks swell to their full height and size. There are two advantages in blanching Rhubarb: first, the desirable qualities of appearance and flavor; and secondly, a saving in the quantity of sweetening material to render them agreeable to the taste. The stalks, when blanched, are more tender than when grown under the influence of strong light and in open situations.

Culture in cold or hot latitudes.—There is no obstacle to the cultivation of this interesting plant. It will stand unprotected as far north as the St. Lawrence, and yield annually a large crop. North of that limit all that is necessary for its preservation is to throw over it, during Winter, a quantity of dry leaves, to keep off intense frost, and, as Spring opens, to clear away the litter and cultivate the ground, as previously directed. If there is three months of good sun, it is all the plant requires to mature it. Wherever Oats will grow, the Rhubarb will thrive; only give it depth of soil for its roots, and manure to stimulate its luxuriance. In southern latitudes it must be planted in moist situations, and under the shade of buildings, to ward off the scorching rays of the sun at mid-day, and in dry periods it must be watered freely. The whole of this continent, from the Gulf of Mexico to Hudson's Bay, may enjoy the luxury of this vegetable.

Its cultivation may be pursued to any extent for its root for medicinal purposes. In such a case, the species *Undulatum* and *Palmatum* should be planted two by four feet apart. They should not be robbed of their leaves at any period of their growth. After the roots have been seven years under culture, they are then ready to be lifted. After being washed thoroughly and deprived of their small fibres, cut the strong roots into pieces about two inches long, and these pieces lengthwise. Thread them on cords and hang them up to dry. These cords should be turned upside down every day for a week, to prevent the juice settling in any one part of the root. They should not be laid on boards to dry, for the board will absorb a portion of the juice, depriving the roots of so much of their strength We doubt not but it may thus be dried as perfectly in this country as in any of those where it is cultivated for export.

SALSAFY, OR VEGETABLE OYSTER.

Tragopògon pòrifolius.—Salsifis, Fr.

Salsafy is a hardy carrot-rooted biennial, a native of the mountain meadows of Switzerland. It is considered wholesome and nutricious, and much esteemed by some classes, under the name of Oyster-plant, from its flavor after being cooked, having a considerable resemblance to the Oyster. It makes an excellent variety at the table, and forms an agreeable dish throughout the Winter season. As the Oyster is a very celebrated fish, and many in the interior rarely obtain it, all may cultivate this vegetable, which really makes a near approach to it in taste, when cooked in the following manner. Previous to boiling the roots, let them be slightly scraped, and then laid in water for about an hour; then boil them till quite tender. Let them be taken out and laid to drain for a short time, during which a thick batter should be made with the white of eggs beaten up with a little flour. Grate the roots down tolerably fine; press them into small flattened balls; dip these in the batter, and roll them into grated crackers or crumbs of bread; then fry them in a pan till they are of a deep brown color, when they are ready for the table, and will form a very agreeable and even delicious dish.

Culture.—Sow the seed in drills, half an inch deep, and ten inches apart, in April, or before the end of May. As soon as the plants are an inch high, thin them out with the hoe to four or six inches apart. Keep the ground clear of weeds, giving them the general culture of Carrots. This vegetable is perfectly hardy, and may stand out all Winter, though it is necessary to store away a quantity for Winter use when the ground is hard frozen. They like a deep, rich soil, and will be in good condition for the table till the end of March.

SCORZONERA.

Scorzonèra hispánica.—Scorzonere, Fr.

This vegetable is a native of Spain, and has, to a limited extent, been long in cultivation. There is very little difference between the character and flavor of this root and that of Salsafy. It is cultivated more as a variety than for any real utility as a vegetable. It is cooked in the same manner as the former, and cultivated with the Carrot. The seed must be sown in April, as it requires longer to mature than either the Salsafy or the Carrot.

SEA-KALE.

Crámbe Marítima.—Chou Marin, Fr.—*Meerkohl*, Ger

THIS plant is found growing on the sea-coasts of Europe particularly in England, where it is cultivated to a very great extent in the gardens of the wealthy. It is closely related to the Cabbage, and professional men have observed that all the good qualities of that family are centred in the Sea-Kale. I suspect this opinion would be contested by lovers of "Corned Beef and Cabbage;" however, I have no doubt that a free use of this vegetable and Rhubarb, in the Spring, would contribute greatly to reduce the Doctor's account. It can be obtained with very little trouble, the whole Winter, in its most perfect state; but the fact of its having to be attended to in these dreary months, retards its progress. The tillers and workers of the soil, independent of their nocturnal slumbers, very frequently slumber with nature, and are inert at any employment that requires their peculiar care at that period of the year.

The mode of dressing this vegetable for the table is as follows: Tie the stalks, or rather clusters of stalks, in bundles, and boil them with plenty of water, and a little salt, for twenty minutes, observing that the water is boiling before they are put in. Have a toast ready, dip it in the water, put it on the dish, and the Sea-Kale upon it, and pour a little white sauce over it, consisting of cream or milk, thickened with flour and butter; or simply cook it as Asparagus is done, which it much resembles.

CULTURE.—We venture to assert that no culinary vegetable can be raised either naturally or artificially with less trouble or a greater certainty of success than the Sea-Kale, as in either case the plants will last many years; and in their periodical forcing they give the gardener no anxiety, as the desired result is certain. Sow the seed thinly, in drills one inch deep, and twelve apart, at any time in March or April (one ounce of seed will be sufficient for a moderate family). If the weather be dry, water it freely. In about two or three weeks the plants will appear; thin them out to an inch apart; and when they have attained more strength, thin them out to two or three inches. They require no further care the first season, except to hoe freely and keep clear of weeds. During November, cover the crowns of the plants with a few inches of earth. Early in the following Spring, prepare a piece of rich, sandy ground, well manured, about ten feet by thirty, giving it twenty-five pounds of salt, and digging the ground fully fifteen inches deep. Mark it out into two four-feet beds, leaving an alley between. In the centre of each bed a line should be drawn, where the strongest plants, after being carefully taken up, are to be planted at two feet apart, taking care that the crown of the plant is set two inches below the surface of the bed, to allow for the future rising of the crowns, which they are inclined to do every year; they will, if judiciously managed, continue in perfection twelve or fifteen years. Within six inches of the edge of each bed, plant other rows in the same manner; thus each bed will contain about forty-five plants. If the season proves very dry, water occasionally, frequently stir the earth and constantly destroy weeds. Do not allow any of the plants to go to seed, which will cause them to grow stronger for the required purpose. Particularly for forcing under pots this is the most general method, and one which will bring this vegetable to perfection. Its season will be from Christmas to April, if the following process is strictly adhered to:

When the number of roots are determined upon for forcing, clear them of all decayed leaves. Early in November, give the bed two inches of well decomposed dung; fork it in lightly, which will strengthen the roots and accelerate their growth. Cover the crowns of the plants three or four inches thick, with any light, sandy soil, or, if convenient, pure sand. After being thus finished, cover the crowns with large pots or boxes, sink ing them one or two inches in the ground, and carefully stopping up any holes in them, to prevent the entrance of any rank steam. When that is done, procure a quantity of leaves from the woods, and mix them with about a fourth or a half of warm, stable-manure; with this cover the whole of the ground and the pots to the depth of twenty inches, which will be quite sufficient to bring this vegetable to a full growth for use, if the temperature of 50° to 60° can be maintained. In very severe weather, over this covering throw some dry litter or boards. If the materials are properly managed, they will come to a heat in two or three weeks; in three or four weeks more, examine a pot or two, and when the plants are found to have sprouts from six to eight inches in length, they may be cut for use, which is to be done by first removing a part of the earth from round the head of the plant, and cutting close to the crown, with part of it adhering, but taking care not to disturb the young shoots that appear round it. Afterwards cover the crowns with earth, as at first, and replace the pots, leaves, and other materials. The plants will remain in a vigorous state of growth for six or eight weeks, by which time the pots may be removed. As the cold weather goes off, take gradually away the covering, as the root and crown, by being forced, would probably be injured by the change, were the entire covering taken away at once. When the plants are finally cleared, level down the earth or sand, and dig in a few inches of the decayed material, which will strengthen the plant for a vigorous growth throughout the season; and they will be found in a good state for forcing in the following Winter.

The plants that are not forced should be covered early in Spring with eight or ten inches of sand, or fine, light soil. They will produce strong sprouts, and be found, on clearing the ground round them, to be finely blanched, of a clear. white color, and when dressed, nearly equal to those blanched under pots. It is admitted that forcing improves the flavor of this esculent It will be found that from a garden with two good beds of this valuable vegetable, it can be enjoyed from January to May, by giving the simple attention we have detailed.

Besides the above method of forcing, it can be done successfully in pits, frames, or hot-houses, where these erections are in use. Put the plants in large pots, using earth of a light, rich nature. Place them in any dark corner, where, with a little moisture at times, they will bring good sprouts for the table.

SHALLOT.

A'llium ascalŏnicum.—*Eschalote*, Fr.—*Schallote*, Ger.

It will be observed from the botanic name of Shallot, that it is classed with the Onion tribe. It was introduced from Ascalon, a town of Syria, and frequently is known under the name of Eschalots. They have a strong but not unpleasant odor, and are preferred to the Onion for various purposes of cookery and seasoning. Many epicures consider them the best seasoning for a good old-fashioned dish of beef-steaks. Though it has been two hundred years in cultivation, very little of the article is used in this country, unless by the French.

Culture.—The roots are bulbous, and increase readily by offsets, the largest of which are most proper for use. The bulbs are oblong and irregular, seldom becoming large; generally growing in clusters, they do not swell like roots that grow singly. The soil best adapted for their growth is a light, rich, sandy loam, though they will thrive well in any rich soil that is not saturated with moisture. Plant them in October or November, in drills, six inches apart, three inches deep, and about eight inches from row to row. If a quantity of soot be mixed with the soil, it will greatly prevent the attacks of a maggot, which frequently commits depredations upon this plant. Early in Spring draw away the earth from the bulbs,

6

leaving them entirely naked; nothing further is required than to keep them free from weeds. In July the tops begin to turn yellow, when the roots can be taken up and dried in the same manner as Garlic. If the planting is delayed till Spring, the bulbs will not require to be put under ground, but merely planted as Onion sets, which their culture very much resem-

---

SKIRRET.

Sium Sisarum.—*Chervis*, Fr.—*Zuckerwurzel*, Ger.

SKIRRET is considered a nutricious vegetable, and would be more generally cultivated were it not for the large space of ground required to raise a quantity for general use. It is a perennial plant, a native of Asia, and has been cultivated in Europe about two hundred years. The roots are composed of long, fleshy tubers, joined together in the crown or head. They are cooked like Salsafy, and form a very white, sweet, and pleasant vegetable.

CULTURE.—Soil suitable for the Carrot will also grow this root in perfection. Sow the seeds thinly, in drills, half an inch deep and ten inches wide, at any time from the middle of April to the first of May, the ground having been previously well dug and manured. Sow a few Radish seeds in the drills, to distinguish them, and admit of hoeing to destroy the weeds, lest they overgrow the crop. In five or six weeks they can be thinned out with the hoe to five or six inches apart. Nothing more will be requisite, excepting a constant stirring of the soil and keeping down weeds. About the first of November the roots will be fit for use, and continue so till Spring. On the approach of severe frost, they should be taken up, cleaned and stowed away, like other roots, in sand or dry earth.

SPINACH, OR SPINAGE.

Spinăcia olerăcea.—Epinard, Fr.—*Spinat,* Ger.

THIS vegetable is a hardy annual, said to be a native of Spain, and has been cultivated to a considerable extent for many years. If eaten freely, it is of a laxative and cooling nature, but does not afford much nutriment. It is admitted to be innocent in its effects in all kinds of diseases, and allowed by medical men to be eaten when other vegetables are denied. The leaves of the plants, being of a very succulent or moist nature, must be boiled about ten minutes in a very small portion of water, in which a gentle handful of salt has been put. As it boils, clear off the scum which arises. Drain it well in a colander, season it with butter and pepper, or dress with eggs and vinegar. There are three varieties of Garden Spinach in cultivation, which differ in the size and shape of the leaves, and the greater or less prickliness of the seeds.

Prickly-Seeded, or *Winter Spinach,* is the best for sowing in September for Winter crops.

Round-Seeded is preferred for Spring sowing; and in mild latitudes it is generally used. It produces a rounder, fuller, and more fleshy leaf.

Flanders Spinach.—This is a prickly-seeded variety, having great breadth of foliage. It is more luxuriant and of a greener color. It is not in general use, but deserves special attention.

CULTURE.—This vegetable is generally sown broad-cast, as it is easier performed—a system we deprecate, as being unprofessional, without neatness, and giving afterwards more labor to keep clean. Sow very thinly in drills a quarter of an inch deep, and nine inches from row to row. For Winter and early Spring crops, sow about the end of August, and again about the middle of September. For early Summer crops, sow about the end of March, and, frequently, to the middle of May It succeeds in any common garden soil, but the more it has been previously enriched with manure, the better. Indeed it will not produce its large, expansive leaves, nor fully develope its extraordinary growth, unless highly nurtured. It is a rank grower, and consequently a gross feeder. Always select an open situation, avoiding the vicinity of trees or buildings. If the ground is light and dry, it should be trodden down firmly, or rolled with a roller. The Spring crops can be sown very conveniently between Peas, or on ground where the Pole Beans are intended to be planted. The crop must be well hoed and faithfully cultivated, which draws the moisture to the roots, encouraging the growth. Where the ground is in proper condition, the plants may stand nine inches apart, and the crop will be easily gathered; but if the ground is poor and the plants stinted, the produce is nearly worthless. The seeds will come up in from ten days to two weeks. Thin out the plants when too thick; if they have three or four leaves an inch broad, they may be used till the main crop is sufficiently thinned. When the plants have leaves two or three inches broad, they will be fit for gathering, which is done by croping the outer leaves, the root and heart remaining to shoot out again. We have seen leaves of the Round and Flanders Spinach two feet in circumference. In this vicinity, the Winter Spinach has generally a very thin layer of straw or other light covering laid over it, which greatly protects the roots and prevents their being thrown out by the frost. Gardeners who have any emulation, endeavor to cover a portion of their most advanced crop with mats, or any covering that they can take off in mild weather. This enables them to procure a dish of this vegetable at any period during the Winter months. We would further observe, that if this crop is not kept quite thin, but one plant allowed to touch its neighbor, they will draw up and speedily run to seed. Two ounces of seed will plant five drills, each forty feet long

SQUASH.

Cucùrbita Melópepo.—Courge ou Potiron, Fr.

This vegetable is in general use from June to August, or even October, and is extensively cultivated in this vicinity for the market. There is no garden, however unpretending, should omit its culture.

They may be cooked in the very simplest form, requiring about an hour's boiling in water. When done, mash well, place them in a colander and press out the water freely. Season with pepper, cream and butter, and dish them up for the table.

There are several sorts for both Summer and Winter use The former only deserves attention, as the latter are inferior to the *Cashaw Pumpkin.*

Early Bush, or *Patty-pan*, from its dwarf habit and productiveness, is preferred for early crops. It is of a yellowish white color, round and pan-shaped. Many acres of them are grown for our markets.

Green Striped, or *Large-Green.*—This crook-necked variety is perfectly green, with a few light stripes in it. Some prefer it to the former, though not generally, it being both later and more rampant in growth.

Culture.—Plant in May, June, and July, in hills four feet each way, in the same manner as directed for Cucumbers. Their general management and after-culture is the same in every respect. Half an ounce of seed will supply any family. They are fit for use when about the size of the fist. When the skin becomes so hard that the nail of the finger cannot pierce it easily, it is unfit for use.

SWISS CHARD, OR SILVER BEET.

Béta Vulgàris argentèa.—Swiss Chard, Ger.

THIS spinaceous plant is becoming very generally distributed as a vegetable. Its leaves only are used. It is a variety of the Beet, having bright green foliage, with the leaf-stalk and mid-rib of a pure white, and is sometimes known under the name of *Seakale Beet*, from the fact that the footstalk and nerves of the leaves can be used like that vegetable. The leaf, after being deprived of the strong membranes, is cooked like Spinach, and very favorably received at the table. The root portion of the plant is not generally made use of.

CULTURE.—This is accomplished in the same manner and by the same process as detailed for the Beet, page 28. It is extensively cultivated in France, Germany, and Switzerland. To those who are fond of a vegetable diet, it may form a very prominent portion in the months of June, July, and August—the warm season, when Spinach and Seakale cannot be obtained. Sow for the first crop in March, and for the second in May. An ounce of seed will supply a large family.

TARRAGON.

Artemésia Dracúnculus.—L'Estragon, Fr.—*Dragun,* Ger.

TARRAGON is a perennial plant, a native of Siberia and Tartary, where it is covered during the Winter months with snow. The French are particularly fond of it in salads. The leaves and young tops are used as ingredients in pickles, and a simple infusion of them in vinegar makes an excellent fish sauce; the leaves are also eaten with beef-steaks, having a fragrant smell and an aromatic taste.

Culture.—It is propagated by parting the roots in Spring and planting them in a light, rich soil, one foot apart, but free from dung that is not thoroughly decomposed. Six plants will supply a family. Cover them in severe Winters with rough litter, or a few branches and leaves. If they are planted in moist soil, heavy and continued frosts will destroy their roots; they delight in a warm, dry situation.

THYME.

Thymus vulgàris.—Thym, Fr.—*Thimian*, Ger.

The common garden Thyme is a low, evergreen, procumbent shrub. It is a native of England, Spain and Greece. It has an agreeable aromatic smell, and a warm, pungent taste. Its culinary use is principally for soups and seasoning of every description.

Culture.—A few bushes of this plant is all that is necessary for a family. They can be procured by the slip or division of the root, or from seeds; the latter are very small, and should be sown in moist weather, on a spot of fine soil; cover the seed very lightly and press it with the back of the spade. A spot of ground one foot square is sufficient. Thyme that is intended for Winter use should be cut when just coming into bloom, tied up in bundles, dried in the shade, and put away in paper.

TOMATO.

Solànum Lycopèrsicum.—Tomate, Fr.—*Liebes Apfel*, Ger.

In taking a retrospect of the past eighteen years, there is no vegetable on the catalogue that has obtained such popularity in so short a period as the one now under consideration. In

1828–9 it was almost detested; in ten years more every variety of pill and panacea was "extract of Tomato." It now occupies as great a surface of ground as Cabbage, and is cultivated the length and breadth of the country. As a culinary dish it is on every table from July to October. Contiguous to large cities, where a high price is given for the first and earliest supply, the exertions of the experienced market gardener bring every operation to bear on its early maturity. It is brought to the table in an infinite variety of forms, being stewed and seasoned, stuffed and fried, roasted and raw, and in nearly every form palatable to all. It is also made into pickles, catsup, and salted in barrels for Winter use, so that with a few years more experience, we may expect to see it as an every-day dish from January to January. It belongs to the same family as the Potato, and like it is destined to be universally cultivated in all climates where it will mature; and we yet expect to see it grown to an extent in the erections of the wealthy who inhabit colder latitudes, that they too may enjoy this favorite. There are several kinds grown for fancy purposes, but only three sorts for the table: these are,

The large smooth Red.—This is a very recent variety, in every respect similar to the common sort, only being smooth and free from protuberances and indentations.

Large Red.—The sort that is grown by the hundreds of acres for market supply, and is from three to eighteen inches in circumference.

Pear Shaped.—This variety is of a reddish-pink color, very fleshy, contains fewer seeds than the two former sorts, equally as good for stewing, and preferable for pickling, being more firm, and of a better shape.

Cherry Shaped.—This variety is very appropriately named. It is cultivated expressly for pickling, and forms a very beautiful variety.

There are several other fancy sorts, generally of a yellow color, which have an interest to those who are fond of variety

CULTURE.—It is indispensable, in good gardening, to have this popular vegetable fit for the table at the earliest possible period. We therefore advise all to resort to the best and most expeditious means at their command. Hotbeds, in March, are generally used to grow a few hundreds, or thousands, as wants require. Sow the seed very thinly, and cover it slightly. It is generally sure of vegetating, and if the plants come up thickly, they draw and crowd each other. In a few days they will be three or four inches high, requiring to be freely aired, if in a hotbed, at all favorable periods in time of sunshine. As they advance in growth, transplant into other frames, under glass, where they will stand two or three inches apart, to harden and prepare for removal to the open ground. About the first of May select some sheltered spot; plant them three feet apart, by the side of a close fence, or other erection, where they will have the full benefit of the sun the whole day. When they are about a foot high, draw earth to their stems and surround them with branches for support. The earliest plants should have a few inches taken off their tops as soon as they have set their fruit. This will cause them to ripen more rapidly. Where there is plenty of space under glass, it is a good plan to pot a quantity of the plants in April, and encourage their growth by every possible means, transplanting them into the open air as soon as there is a possibility of settled, warm weather, which is generally about the second week in May, in this vicinity.

Those who have not such convenient arrangements as above, can place a small box or large pot, with good rich earth, in their kitchen window, and sow in it a few seeds, about the middle of March or the first of April. By this means they will have the crop ready two or three weeks before those that are sown in the open air. For a general crop, sow about the last week of April, on a sheltered, warm spot of ground, in light, rich soil. If the nights are cold, cover with a little straw or other brush. Keep the plants thin, that they may grow stocky and strong. Transplant about the 20th of May, two feet from plant to plant and three feet from row to row, where they are to remain. The frame in which the Cabbage plants were during Winter, is an excellent spot for these seeds, which may be sown as soon as they are removed, in March. Protect with mats and shutters in cold weather. The seed grows best when it is only very slightly covered. Although great care is taken for its early protection, it is of a very hardy nature, and will lie dormant in the ground all Winter, vegetating in the Spring, as the season advances. In some seasons there is a caterpillar very destructive to the vines, against which the only remedy is picking them off as soon as they appear. For the proper culture of this crop, it is indispensable to have rich ground. That whereon the Winter Spinach was grown will suit, if in good heart.

TRUFFLE.

Tùbera Terræ'a.—*Truffe*, Fr.—*Trüffel*, Ger.

The Truffle is a subterraneous fungus, growing naturally some inches below the surface, in some parts of Italy, France, and even Great Britain. We do not suppose that its cultivation has been attempted in this country, neither are we intimately acquainted with the process of its culture. It has been successfully grown by several individuals in England, who procured the Truffle from where it was found growing, laying it in a somewhat similar situation, either in the vicinity of woods or in the open field. It is a very singular production, combining (in the opinion of naturalists) a flavor of both flesh and vegetable. It is of a globular formation, about the size of a hen's egg, without any roots or fibres. It is sometimes seen of a dark brown color, while at other times it is of a whitish appearance. The surface is uneven and rough, the flesh firm—white when young, but as it becomes old, it approaches black, with light brown veins. Dogs and swine have been trained to search for the Truffle. In Italy it is called Swine's Bread, as these animals are exceedingly fond of them. The Italians tie a cord to the hog's foot and drive him, observing where he roots. The French and English have dogs called Truffle-dogs, trained to scent it out. These dogs point out the spot, by scraping and barking; and the Truffles, which are generally found in clusters, are dug up with a spade. They are used, like the mushroom, in stuffings, gravies, and other high-seasoned preparations, and will keep perfectly sound for several months.

Culture.—They have been successfully cultivated in Germany, France, and England, on which there is a large pamphlet published, to which we refer those who wish information on the subject. We are not acquainted with the manner of their growth, and it is not our habit to detail to others what we do not practically know.

TURNIP.

Brăssica Ràpa.—*Navet*, Fr.—*Steckrübe*, Ger.

The Turnip is a vegetable common to all temperate and cold latitudes. It has been known for 250 years, and has become, in some countries, an extensive field-crop. It is not positively known of what country it is a native. Horticultural and agricultural science has brought it to its present perfection. It is accounted a salubrious root, but in weak stomachs it is apt to produce flatulency and prove difficult of digestion. It is frequently used medicinally in coughs, hoarseness, and other asthmatic disorders. The syrup of Turnip, after being extracted by baking and mixed with honey, is a family receipt for these complaints. Turnips are principally used at the table with boiled meats, or mashed, strained, and mixed with butter, cream, and other seasoning, for which purpose mid-sized Turnips are better than large ones, as the latter, being of a spongy nature, contain more water than those smaller. In the present day, during the great deficiency of the Potato crop, they form a partial substitute for that valuable root—especially in Europe, where some of the finer kinds of the Turnip have been found, by recent analysis, to give nearly as much nourishment. The young sprouts from the tops, in Spring, make excellent greens. There are only a few sorts suitable for garden culture.

Early White Dutch, or *White Strap-leaved*, is a very early kind, of a round, flat form; the leaves are short and narrow. This and the following variety will produce roots fit for the table in six weeks from sowing.

Early Red-top Dutch, or *Strap-leaved Red-top*, has every character of the former, except that the portion of the root which is fully exposed above ground is of a red or purple color.

Early Yellow Dutch is a very beautifully formed variety, of the color indicated by its name. It is quite firm, sweet, round in form, and keeps well.

Of this class there are also the *White* and *Yellow Stone*, *Yellow Malta*, *Snowball*, and some others, all of which we think, in this climate, inferior to the three described.

For Spring use, the following Swede or Rutabaga Turnips should be sown:

The *Purple-topped Swede* is of an oval, tapering form, and requires to be sown in July; flesh very fine, and keeps till Spring.

Improved Swede.—We are highly in favor of this variety of Turnip, either for the garden or field; it has a better formed root than the common sort; the leaves do not grow so strong; the flesh is of a fine yellow, and very pleasant flavor.

The following are the relative nutritive properties of the Swede and Garden or Field Turnips:

4 oz. Swede Turnip afford 110 grs. nutritive matter.

4 oz. Dutch or Garden afford 85 grs. nutritive matter.

Culture.—The soil most genial for the Turnip is acknowledged to be a gravelly, sandy loam. Some say "poor soil, where no other vegetables will grow," is the best: I say, good rich soil, with a dry bottom. In such sow for an early crop as soon as the frost is out of the ground, either broadcast or in drills, ten inches apart and one-fourth of an inch deep. An ounce of seed will sow a bed four feet wide and forty feet long. Rake the surface even. If dry weather, press the ground with the back of the spade or a light wooden roller. One sowing only can be made in the Spring. From the middle to the end of July is the proper time for sowing the Swede or Rutabaga. Drills are most suitable for this sort. Draw them fifteen inches apart, and thin out the plants as they grow, till they stand eight inches from each other. This variety requires very frequent use of the hoe in stirring the soil, to keep it sweet and encourage the growth requisite to mature this best and most nutritious of Turnips. In August sow the other sorts for a Fall and Winter supply. It is best to make two sowings, say about the first and towards the middle or end of the month; roll or tramp firm the ground after the seed at this period of the year—the first sowing to mature early for immediate use, the last sowing to store away for a Winter supply. In some seasons we have to sow, and sow, and sow again, either from drought or the effects of the fly, which frequently destroys it as soon as it vegetates; in dry seasons it is particularly destructive. In garden culture, a few pots of water every evening will promote the growth of the seed, and bring it speedily away from the attacks of the fly. One thing must be observed: to have the ground always fresh dug before sowing. Soot, wood-ashes, and air-slacked lime are all said to be preventives, if strewn over the plants. We feel assured that its application will retard their progress, but cloudy and showery weather is more effectual. If seed of the current year and seed of one or two years old be sown on the same piece of ground separately, the old seed will frequently be cut off, while the seed of the current year will escape. Good seed will germinate in from thirty-six to forty-eight hours. When the crop is destroyed, stir or dig the ground immediately and sow again. When the plants have grown about an inch high, introduce the hoe among them, and thin out to two or three inches apart; and in a week or two more, give them another hoeing and thinning. Till they stand six inches from each other, do not draw any earth to their roots; in fact the reverse was our practice twenty years ago: they were sown on ridges, and the earth drawn down as the plants advanced in growth. The result was frequently forty tons per acre.

TAKING UP THE CROP.—Turnips may be kept perfectly sound till Spring by being taken up about the first of November, or before severe frost sets in. Cut the leaves off to about half an inch from the bulb; collect the latter, and put them in a dry pit or cellar; cover with straw, and earth over all. Thus protected, they will be found fresh and perfect till February, after which the Swede will be fit for the table till April. Those for Spring use can be pitted out of doors in a dry situation, piling them in a conical form and covering them with three inches of straw and a foot or eighteen inches of earth, which will be ample protection. When opened in Spring, these will be found to have nearly all the flavor of being fresh from the field.

SAVE SEED.—In many cases this is very essential; you will then be always sure of the age and quality. Select early in Spring a few of the best formed roots, draw deep drills two feet apart and place the bulbs therein, covering them all over carefully with the earth. They will soon shoot up and branch out, ripening their seeds in July. It is preferable, however to change the seed of this, as well as all other vegetables, every few years; and in purchasing, buy always from a responsible vender, who feels a vital interest in selling a pure and genuine article. The seed will keep three years in a dry place; if it is two years old, soak it in water twenty-four hours before sowing.

VEGETABLE MARROW.

Cucúrbita ovífera, var.—*Patiron*, Fr.

We have been frequently greatly amused by some of our friends kindly presenting us with seeds purporting to be the marrow of all the vegetables, or "Vegetable Marrow." It is a species of Gourd introduced from Persia several years ago, and has been found useful for culinary purposes in every stage of its growth. When young, it is cut in slices and fried with butter; when more mature, it is cut in quarters, stewed in rich gravy, and seasoned to taste; in this way it is very agreeable, and said to be both wholesome and nutritious.

Culture.—This vegetable is characteristically situated between the Pumpkin and the Squash, consequently its habits and mode of growth are very similar to those plants. Plant the seeds in hills, about the first of May, six feet apart, and manage them as directed for the above. It has an oval fruit inside, very fleshy. In saving the seed, keep the plants distant from any of the family.

WATER CRESS.

Sisy'mbrium Nastürtium.—*Cresson de Fontaine,* Fr.—*Brünnenkresse,* Ger.

THE many virtues that were attributed to the Water Cress in days of old, if at all applicable then, are equally valuable at the present day. Its botanical name alludes to its warm and cordial qualities, which were considered to infuse life into persons of low and dull spirits. The Cress is also famed for its antiscorbutic qualities, and may be safely eaten at all seasons of the year, but is particularly in request in Spring. It should be found in our markets in profusion, being peculiarly adapted to the constitutions of those who live chiefly on animal food. Water Cresses are found growing in clear runs of water and springs throughout this country and Europe. There is about an acre of them at Spring-Mill, near this city. It is a plant that has winged leaves, like the Rose, or like half-grown leaves of the Ash tree, of a roundish heart-like shape, with few indentures on the edges; the upper part of which, after more mature growth, is of a reddish-brown color, and forms roots in the water at every joint.

CULTURE. Wherever there is a running stream and a gravelly soil, they may be cultivated to advantage. In fact every spring house in the country should have attached to it a bed of Water Cresses. They may be obtained by the simple process of throwing the plants on the water; the seeds will ripen and soon propagate in abundance. They can also be cultivated in low, moist, loamy soil, that can be irrigated and drained at pleasure. Give it a deep diging with the spade in March or April; make beds four feet wide, and set the plants therein at about six inches apart. Water them abundantly; they will soon establish themselves, and the only culture they require is to keep them moist, and destroy carefully every weed. In the absence of moisture the plants will be destroyed by the heat and drought. There are also the

AMERICAN CRESS,

Barbarèa præcox.—*Cresson de Amerique*, Fr.—*Amerikanisher Kresse*, Ger.; and the

WINTER CRESS,

Ery'simum Barbarèa,—*Cresson de Terre*, Fr.—*Winter Kresse*, Ger.;

But both of these are subordinate to the *Water Cress* in every character, and our pages may be occupied with more useful subjects.

CLOSING REMARKS ON VEGETABLES.

Through these few pages I have endeavored to inculcate upon the student the benefit of being always *in time* with a crop. Never delay doing to-day, in the hope of having more time to-morrow. Do it at once, if it can be done. Gardeners have not a moment to spare—unoccupied ground, weeds, hoeing, raking, sowing, reaping, digging—preparing poles, rods, stakes, manure, and many other duties, demand his attention at all times. We have never seen a good gardener who did not feel it a pleasure to be in advance of these wants. Get once behind, lose time, and it is hard to make up. Sow early in the season, and if you fail you have time for a second trial; whereas, if you sow late and miss your crop, the opportunity of recovering the loss is gone with it. Sow before or just after rain, but never when the ground is wet. Beware of sowing deep, or in dry weather, or on dry ground. If this cannot be avoided, soak your seeds in water a few hours, sow them, and then water the ground freely. ☞ *Gardeners never sleep when the sun is up.*

MEDICINAL HERBS

The following is a list of such plants as are generally denominated Medicinal Herbs, and which are found to be more or less wanted in most families. We therefore give a short description of them, and the purposes for which they are most commonly used. They may, in most instances, be very easily cultivated. The soil for growing the greater part should be light and dry, but that of a poorer description is more suitable for some, as Lavender, Rosemary, Rue, Sage, Wormwood, and a few others; and if planted in a rich, moist soil, much of their aromatic quality flies off, and they are rendered less capable of withstanding any severe weather.

ANGELICA.

Angélica archangélica.—*Angelique*, Fr.—*Engelwürtz*, Ger.

Is a native of the northern parts of Europe, and has been long cultivated. It is biennial, and propagated from its seeds, which are to be sown as soon as gathered, in August, in a moist situation; and when the plants are about six inches high, they must be transplanted to a similar soil, about three feet apart. The plants will last many years, provided they are not allowed to run to seed. The flowering stems should be cut down when a few inches high. The stalks of Angelica were formerly blanched, and eaten as Celery, but they are now only used as a sweetmeat, when candied, by the confectioners. The Laplanders extol the utility of this herb for coughs and other disorders of the chest, but in this country it is seldom employed for that purpose, as many other simples surpass it in aromatic and carminative powers.

ANISE-SEED.

Pimpinélla Anìsum.—Boucage, Fr.—*Anis*, Ger.

A native of Egypt and some other eastern countries. The seeds are annually imported from Malta, and Spain. The plant is annual, and propagated by sowing the seed in a light, dry soil, in Spring. Anise-seeds have a warm, aromatic smell, and a pleasant, warm taste, accompanied with a degree of sweetness; they have been useful in many complaints, but none more so than in flatulent colics and obstructions of the breast, for diarrhœas, and for strengthening the tone of the stomach in general.

BALM.

Melíssa officinàlis.—Melisse, Fr.—*Melisse*, Ger.

So called from the Greek word signifying *honey*, because of the abundant and excellent honey of its flowers, for which bees greatly frequent it. The Garden Balm is a native of the mountains of Geneva, Savoy, and Italy. It is perennial, and may be readily propagated by parting the roots in Spring or Autumn, and planting them in beds of common garden mould. The herb, in its recent state, has a weak, aromatic tāste, and a pleasant smell, somewhat of the lemon kind. Balm was formerly esteemed of great use in all complaints supposed to proceed from a disordered state of the nervous system. As tea, however, it makes a grateful dilutent drink in fevers, and in this way it is commonly used either by itself or acidulated with lemons.

BLESSED THISTLE.

Centaurèa benedícta.—Centaurée Sudorifique, Fr.—*Cardo benedicten*, Ger.

A NATIVE of the south of France, Spain, and the Levant. It is annual, and propagated from seed sown in Autumn. This plant has obtained the name of Benedictus, or Blessed, from its supposed extraordinary medicinal qualities. It has an intensely bitter taste and disagreeable smell. It was formerly employed to assist the operation of emetics; but the flowers of Chamomile are now substituted for it with equal advantage. It was also thought, when taken internally, to be peculiarly efficacious in malignant fevers. In loss of appetite, where the stomach has been injured by irregularities, its good effects have been frequently experienced. It has now lost much of its reputation, and does not seem to be essentially different from other simple bitters.

BORAGE.

Boràgo officinàlis.—Bourrache, Fr.—*Borragen*, Ger.

THIS herb is said to have originated from Aleppo, but is now naturalized in many parts of Europe. It is a hardy annual, and easily cultivated, from sowing the seeds in April, which come up without any care. Borage is cultivated in our gardens on account of the supposed cordial virtues of its flowers, but they have long lost their reputation. In Italy its young and tender leaves are in common use, both as a pot-herb and a salad. In France its flowers, with those of *Nasturtium*, are put into salads as an ornament. In England it is now nearly neglected, but the flowers and upper leaves are sometimes used as an ingredient in that Summer beverage composed of wine, water, lemon juice, and sugar, called a cool tankard, to which they seem to give an additional coolness.

CARAWAY.

Carum Cárui.—Carvi, Fr.—*Kummel*, Ger.

A native of many countries in the northern parts of Europe. It is biennial, and propagated by sowing the seeds in Spring The seeds of this plant are well known to have a pleasant, spicy smell, and a warm, aromatic taste; and on that account they are much used as a common ingredient in cakes, and are encrusted in sugar for comfits; they are also distilled with spirituous liquors, to improve their flavor. The tender leaves in Spring are sometimes boiled in soups.

CHAMOMILE.

A'nthemis nóbilis.—Camomille, Fr.—*Kamille*, Ger.

Grows wild in many parts of Europe. It is a hardy perennial, and easily propagated by parting the roots early in Spring. Both the leaves and flowers of the Chamomile have a strong, though not ungrateful, smell, and a very bitter, nauseous taste. The flowers possess the stomachic and tonic qualities usually ascribed to simple bitters. A watery infusion of them is frequently used for the purpose of exciting vomiting, or for promoting the operation of emetics. They are very generally used in emollient decoctions, to assuage pain; and externally as fomentations.

CLARY.

Sálvia Sclàrea.—Orvale, Fr.—*Scharlachkraut*, Ger.

A NATIVE of Italy and Syria, and long known in the English garden, where it is a hardy biennial. It is easily raised from seed, which should be sown in March, in any bed or border of common earth. Clary was formerly much used in cookery, but it is not now in much repute. A wine is sometimes made from the herb in flower, which has a flavor not unlike Frontigniac.

CORIANDER.

Coriándrum Satìvum.—Coriandre, Fr.—*Koriander*, Ger.

A NATIVE of the southern parts of Europe, and of China. It is a hardy annual, and propagated from seed sown in Autumn, in an open situation, on a bed of good, fresh earth. The dried seeds of Coriander have a tolerably grateful smell, with a moderately warm and slightly pungent taste. They are carminative (soothing or softening) and stomachic; and are commonly sold by the confectioners, encrusted with sugar.

DILL.

Anèthum gravèolens.—L'Anith, Fr.—*Dill*, Ger.

GROWS wild among the corn in Spain and Portugal; and may be produced by sowing the seeds soon after they are ripe, in any light soil. The seeds of Dill have a moderately warm, pungent taste, and an aromatic smell, but not of the most agreeable kind; they were formerly much used in medicine, but are now seldom employed. They are sometimes put into pickles to heighten the flavor, particularly of Cucumbers.

ELECAMPANE.

I'nula Helènium.—*Inule,* Fr.—*Inule,* Ger.

The Elecampane is a strong-growing perennial plant, a native of Britain, rising from three to five feet high. It is cultivated in most gardens, and delights in a moist or shaded situation. It can be propagated by dividing the root in the Autumn. The roots are thick, Carrot-shaped, and aromatic; when dried, ground, and made into a tea, it is considered an excellent remedy for a cold. In some countries the root is candied and used as a stomachic for strengthening the tone of the viscera.

HOREHOUND.

Marrúbium vulgàre.—*Marrúbe,* Fr.

Common in many parts of the world, on waste ground, and among rubbish, in hot, dry, and dusty situations. The plant is annual, and may be raised by sowing the seeds in any of the Spring months. The leaves have a moderately strong smell, of the aromatic kind, but not agreeable; their taste is very penetrating, bitter, and durable in the mouth. This herb was extolled by the ancients for its efficacy in removing obstructions of the lungs. It has been chiefly employed in humoral asthmas, obstinate coughs, and pulmonary consumptions. Its use is also said to be beneficial in affections of the liver. Lozenges made of the juice of this herb and sugar are esteemed good for colds. Though Horehound possesses some share of medicinal power, its virtues do not appear to be clearly ascertained, and it is now rarely prescribed by physicians.

HYSSOP.

Hyssopus officinalis.—Hysope, Fr.—*Isop*, Ger.

A NATIVE of the south of Europe, and must have been known among the ancients. This plant, being perennial, is easily propagated, by sowing the seeds in a border of light mould, in the Spring season, or by slips, and cutting and parting the roots. The whole plant has a strong aromatic scent, and the leaves and flowers are of a warm, pungent taste; they are sometimes reduced to powder and used with cold salad herbs. Hyssop has the general virtues ascribed to aromatics, and is recommended in asthmas, coughs, and other disorders of the lungs. The young leafy shoots and flower-spikes are usually employed, being cut as they are wanted. The flower stems may be cut during the Summer, and tied up in bunches for use.

LAVENDER.

Lavándula Spica.—Lavande, Fr.—*Spiklavendel*, Ger.

Is a very hardy plant, and a native of the south of Europe. It may be readily increased by planting slips or cuttings of the young shoots in the Spring. The common Lavender has been cultivated for ages past. The fragrant smell of the flower is well known, and to most persons is very agreeable; to the taste it is bitterish, warm, and somewhat pungent; the leaves are weaker, and less grateful. The flowers are often employed as a perfume, and medicinally as mild stimulants and corroborants, in several complaints, both internally and externally. They are also sometimes used in the form of a conserve

PENNY-ROYAL MINT.

Méntha Pulègium.—*Pouliot*, Fr.—*Polcy*, Ger.

Is a native of watery places. It is easily propagated by parting the roots in Spring. They succeed best in a strong, moist soil, and when planted on the edges of rivulets, ponds, &c. Penny-royal has a warm, pungent flavor, somewhat similar to Mint, but more acrid, and less agreeable both in taste and smell. It possesses the general properties of other mints, but is supposed to be of less efficacy as a stomachic. This herb is less frequently used now for medicinal purposes than formerly.

PEPPERMINT.

Méntha labitàta.—*Menthe*, Fr.—*Munze*, Ger.

A native of watery places in various parts of the world This variety has a more penetrating smell than any of the other Mints, and a much stronger and warmer taste. It may be increased with facility by young offset plants or shoots, or by parting the roots in Spring, or by planting cuttings during any of the Summer months, in a moist soil. Peppermint is much cultivated for medicinal purposes, as well as for distillation; its stomachic and carminative qualities render it useful in flatulent cholics, hysteric affections, and retchings, in which it acts as a cordial. The Essence of Peppermint was formerly considered an elegant medicine; and a cordial is made from this plant which is by many people much admired.

ROSEMARY.

Rosemarìnus officinàlis.—*Romarin*, Fr.—*Rosmarin*, Ger.

A NATIVE of the south of Europe, the Levant, and found occasionally in the Grecian isles. It is propagated from the seed, or by planting slips or cuttings in the early Spring months. Rosemary has a fragrant aromatic smell, and a warm, pungent taste; the leaves and tender tops are the strongest; the flowers, by themselves, are much weaker but more agreeable. This herb is reckoned one of the most powerful of those plants which stimulate and corroborate the nervous system; it has, therefore, been recommended in various affections supposed to proceed from debilities. It is generally given in the form of an infusion.

RUE.

Rùta gravèolens.—*Rue*, Fr.—*Rante*, Ger.

Is a hardy shrub, and a native of the south of Europe. It is propagated in a similar manner to the Rosemary, and requires the same cultivation. The common Rue has a strong, ungrateful odor, and a bitter, hot, penetrating taste. The leaves are so acrid as to irritate and inflame the skin if they are much handled. Rue was much used by the ancients, who ascribed to it many excellent qualities. It is employed by some as a tea, and also externally, in various kinds of fomentations. A conserve, made by beating the fresh leaves with thrice their weight of sugar, is the most commodious form for using the herb in substance. It is a powerful astringent, and adapted to phlegmatic habits, or weak and hysterical constitutions suffering from retarded or obstructive secretions.

SAGE.

Sálvia officinàlis.—Sauge, Fr.—*Salbey*, Ger.

Is a native of the south of Europe, a perennial, and readily increased by planting slips or cuttings in April. Sage has a strong, fragrant smell, and a warm, bitterish, aromatic taste. It was in ancient times considered as a remedy of general efficacy in all diseases. At present, however, few practitioners consider it as an article of much importance in medicine. Although frequently employed as a sudorific, it seems to have no advantage in this respect over many other plants. The Chinese, who are said to have experienced the good effect of Sage, value it highly, and prefer it to their own Tea. The Dutch have long been in the habit of drying Sage leaves in great quantities, and taking them out to China, where for every pound of Sage they get in exchange four pounds of Tea. It is much used in cookery of various descriptions.

SCURVY GRASS.

Cochleària officinàlis.—Cranson officinal, Fr.—*Loffelkraut*, Ger.

COMMON on the sea coasts of Europe, and not unfrequent in mountainous countries, far inland. It is biennial, and propagated from seed sown in the Spring, or by parting the roots and planting them in a light, moist soil. This plant has a warm, acrid, bitter taste, and a pungent, rather unpleasant smell when bruised. It has been considered as one of the most effectual of all the antiscorbutics, when eaten as a salad with Water Cress, &c.

SORREL.

Rùmex acetòsa.—Oseille, Fr.—*Sauerampfer*, Ger.

Some species of the Sorrel is found in every part of the world. Wherever seen, it indicates a poor, sour soil. It is peculiarly a French dish, and considered an effectual remedy against scurvy. Its general use is in salads, and occasionally boiled as a sauce, and may be cooked similarly to Spinach. It is increased by seeds or division of the roots. Plant in a light, rich, moist soil, in rows ten inches apart; they will furnish a plentiful supply of leaves the same season. They afterwards only require to be kept clean, and to have the seed-stems cut down as well as the overgrown leaves in Autumn.

TANSY.

Tanacètum vulgàre.—Tanaise, Fr.—*Rheinfarn*, Ger.

A native of banks, hedges, and borders of fields, in most parts of the middle of Europe. It is perennial, and easily propagated by seed, and also by parting the roots in Spring and planting them in any light soil or situation. Tansy has a strong, aromatic smell, and a bitter taste. It is tonic and stomachic, and has the usual qualities attributed to bitters of the warm or aromatic kind. It was formerly much used in puddings, but has of late been neglected, and is now seldom used, either as a culinary vegetable or medicinal herb.

WORMWOOD.

Artemisia absinthium.—Absinthe, Fr.— *Wermuth,* Ger.

It is a hardy perennial, and may be propagated by slips, in March or October, or raised from seeds sown after they are ripe. The leaves have a strong, offensive smell, and a very bitter, nauseous taste; the flower equally bitter, but less nauseous. Wormwood is a moderately warm stomachic and corroborant, and for these purposes it was formerly in common use, but it has now given place to bitters of a less ungrateful kind. Wormwood was formerly much used by brewers instead of Hops, to give the bitter taste to their malt liquors, and to preserve them. This plant very powerfully resists putrefaction, and is made a principal ingredient in antiseptic fomentations.

APPLICATION OF OUR REMARKS TO VARIOUS PARTS OF THE UNITED STATES.

The word Spring, when applied to the Season, is everywhere known. When thus applied by us in the preceding pages, it is intended to convey to the reader the period of the year when the buds of the earliest trees appear green. *Early in Spring* is indicated by the buds on the trees beginning to swell. *Late in Spring*, when the leaves have put forth.

About Philadelphia, Spring generally begins from the 10th to the 15th of March.

In South Carolina, the northern parts of Georgia and Alabama, Spring begins five weeks earlier than it does with us.

In the southern parts of Virginia and Kentucky, Spring generally opens about the 20th of February.

In Massachusetts and the upper part of New York, Spring opens from the 25th of March to the first of April.

By these observations being kept in view, the details of this work may be made applicable to any part of the United States.

FRUITS.

THIS subject has engrossed the attention of scientific and practical men for the last four hundred years. We do not presume to enter into their speculations and investigations; our object is a much humbler one—to give a few simple and practical hints on the subject of fruit culture, culled from our own experience, and that of one or two individuals upon whose judgment we can place reliance. There are few, even of those who have studied the nature and character of fruits, that, out of their own collection, know, at first sight, many varieties; and such is the diversity of taste, that we greatly question if five individuals out of one hundred could be procured that would agree as to the best six Apples, Pears, Peaches or Grapes. This incongruity entirely disconcerts the inquiring amateur, gardener, or farmer; but the reason of it is evident. The slight differences that distinguish some varieties; the alterative effects that soil has upon the growth and flavor of others; as well as the favorable and unfavorable results from situation, causing trees grafted from the same stock frequently to mature fruits so entirely dissimilar that they are inconsiderately noticed as being something *new*. This desire for new fruit has become such a mania, that it greatly encourages the introduction, both at home and from abroad, of sorts that are worthless, compared with our old well-tried kinds. These are also witheringly discarded by some croakers, who raise the physiological cry of "the old kinds wearing out." This reasoning is not from analogy, but is merely a supposition. It would be a very easy task to renew any worn-out tree, that had only a few fresh and sound buds left; or even to renovate trees that are in a declining state; in the former case by budding or grafting upon young stocks that have been grown from the seed; in the latter, by scraping off the old bark from the trunk and branches, and renewing the soil about the roots. Our object, however, is not to enter into a detail of the causes, effects, and diseases of trees, and their remedies. These subjects are elaborately treated of in the periodicals of the day. Our object is to lay before our readers a really *select* catalogue of *select* fruits, that will be eatable the whole year, from which more pleasure will be derived than by cultivating acres containing trees not two alike, at least in name. We say differing only in name, for the cultivator will find that some fruits are grown under from three to thirty names, so that after selecting with care one hundred kinds of fruit, there may prove to be not fifty distinct, and one-half of these not worth culture. The fruit catalogues of the present day are very imposing bundles of paper and ink, got up to allay the appetite for new fruits. Those whose sole object is to grow for domestic use or for sale, should select such as agree with the climate of the locality, and are known to be both good and productive. Such are those we now introduce, premising that we are under obligations to Mr. Thos. Hancock, an eminent orchardist and nurseryman of Burlington, N. J., both for descriptions of fruits and their characteristic beauties or defects. They are all propagated either by grafting or budding; and as it is our desire that all our readers should know how to propagate, and by what means to perpetuate every variety of fruit we will briefly detail the operations.

Grafting.—Whip or tongue grafting (Fig. 18) is the mode most in use in the best fruit-tree nurseries, and is so called from the manner of cutting both the stock and scion in a sloping direction, on one of their sides, so that when brought together they fit exactly, and thus may be tied together. In former times this species of grafting was performed without a slit or tongue, and in that case the former term was more applicable. Subsequently the slit or tongue has been added, which has given rise to the latter term. "The scion (or shoot, *a*) and stock (or tree, *b*) being cut off obliquely, at corresponding angles as near as the operator can judge, make a slit nearly in the centre of the sloping face of the stock downwards, and a corresponding tongue in the scion upwards—this is called tongueing; the tongue, or wedge-like process, forming the upper part of the sloping face of the scion, is then inserted downwards in the cleft of the stock, the inner barks of both being brought closely to unite on one side, so as not to be displaced by tying, which ought to be done immediately with strong cotton twist, tape, or any thready material, brought in a neat manner several times round the stalk. The next operation is to clay the whole over, an inch thick on every side, from about half an inch below the bottom of the graft to as much over the top of the stock, finishing the whole in a long, oval form, and closing it effectually in every part to exclude air and water, which is the sole object of claying. *Grafting Clay* is very simply made of any heavy loam procured from a depth of the soil that has not been subject to culture, combined with a fourth of droppings from the horse or cow stable, moistened and well beat together with a stick, till perfectly incorporated and tough, allowed to stand for a few days, and then softened for use. These materials are always at command; there are several kinds of grafting wax, but

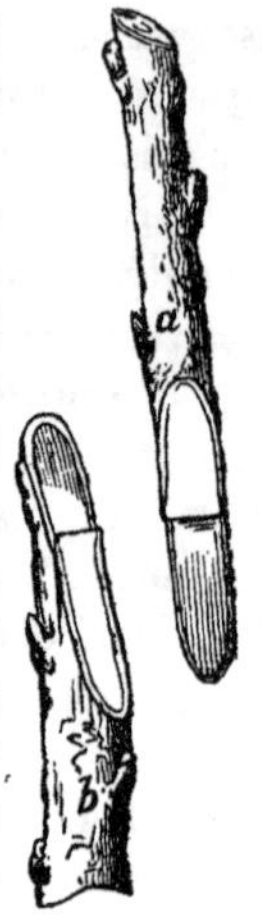

Fig. 18.

they are not so easily prepared, and of no more utility than the clay. Grafting can be performed close to the ground, and earth drawn up round the junction, which will be as serviceable as clay.

Cleft Grafting (Fig. 19) is another method of operating upon large trees, or stocks, where the bark or rind is not too thick. The head of the stock, or branch, being cut off smoothly, a slit is made in the top of the stock with a strong knife or chisel, deep enough to receive the scion, which should be cut sloping, like a wedge, so as to fit the slit made in the stock. The wedge side, which is to be placed outward, is to be made thicker than the other; and in placing the scion into the slit, it must be so adjusted that the rind or inner bark of the scion joins that of the stock; for if these do not unite, the grafts will not succeed. When the stocks are large, two grafts may be put in, (as represented in the figure,) which tie firmly and clay over, as directed for Whip Grafting. As there will be a greater body of clay, in this case, it will be more liable to fall off; it will therefore be necessary to wrap moss, soft hay, or pieces of cloth round the balls, to prevent the rain destroying them. There are many other methods of grafting, all on the same principle differently applied. Some of our amateur correspondents, particularly John A. Crawford, Esq., of Columbia, S. C., takes large limbs two or three inches in diameter, and five to ten feet long, and grafts them into other stocks. These limbs produce fruit the same season. Root grafting is also practised to a considerable extent. Trees and stocks for grafting upon should always be fully established before being operated upon, having had at least one season's growth. Farmers may graft in every field and hedge-row, and by every fence-rail. Fruit trees require no more room than the cumberers of the ground in the shape of saplings, briars, and thorns. Fruits make an ample return.

Fig. 19.

while the latter requires food for which they do not pay. There is no garden or farm but should have a few reserve Plum, Pear, Apple, Peach, Cherry and Quince stocks, on which they can place any sort of fruit they wish to preserve and multiply. These can be readily procured by sowing a few seeds, or planting a few pits, every year. Stone fruit, such as the Cherry, Peach and Plum, do best by budding. Apples and Pears do well by both grafting and budding. Budding is performed as follows:

Budding.—The operation may be performed with any sharp, thin-bladed knife, though one called a "budding-knife," with a thin ivory handle, is best for the purpose. It should be inserted about half an inch above the bud, and passing about one-fourth of the way through the wood of the shoot, come out again about the same distance below it, the cut being as clean as possible. The portion of the bark in the centre of which the bud is situated is called the shield; and when removed, it contains a portion of the wood, which is to be carefully removed with the point of the knife, as shown in Fig. 20; if the wood is dry, and does not separate readily, it is a sign the bud is too old, and it should be rejected.

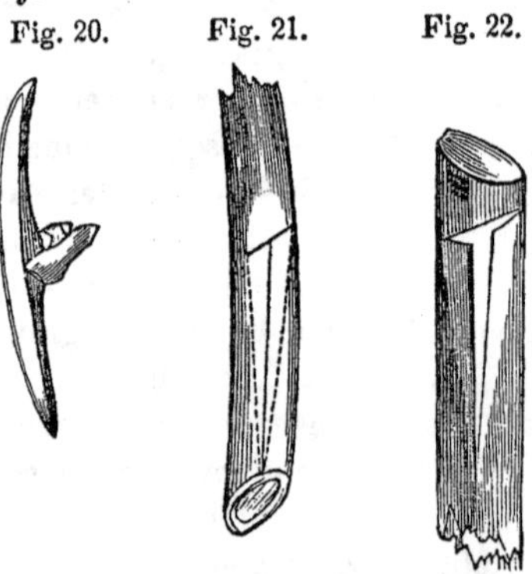
Fig. 20. Fig. 21. Fig. 22.

When the wood is too old or too young, the shield may be taken off only about one-eighth of the way through the shoot, and inserted into the stock without removing the portion of the wood it contains: this method, particularly with very young shoots, is very successful. If it is necessary to transport the buds to some distance, this may be safely done by cutting a portion of the shoot, and, after cutting off the foliage, wrap them up in damp moss, a few large leaves, or wet paper, when they may be kept for three or four days. In applying the bud to the stock, an incision is to be made lengthwise through the bark (but not so as to injure the wood), about an inch in length; and this is to be diagonally crossed at the top by another incision, as shown in Fig. 21. The thin ivory handle, or back of the knife, should then be used to raise the bark, as shown in Fig. 22, and the shield inserted within, gently pressing it to the bottom of the perpendicular incision. When it is properly placed, the portion of it above the diagonal cross should be cut off, as in Fig. 23, and great care should be taken that the bud is in close contact with the wood of the stock. When this is done, bind it up with damp matting, or cotton twist, all except the bud, (see Fig. 24,) which must be left free to the air, but protected from the powerful action of the sun or wet, either of which would defeat the whole operation. In two weeks the success or failure will be known, when the bandages must be loosened, though not entirely taken away. From July to the middle of September budding may be done, choosing always cloudy weather, or a few days after a heavy rain; but, for limited operations, any evening may be chosen, always following the indication of the free parting of the wood from the bark; for if the bark does not rise with facility, the buds are liable to perish for want of a due supply of nourishment. The buds should always be selected from vigorous young wood, that has nearly done growing. Cut off the leaves, allowing about half an inch of the footstalk to remain

Fig. 23.

Fig. 24.

for the convenience of inserting the buds. Early in the ensuing Spring, the stocks on which those buds are that have taken, should be headed down to within two inches of the bud, which will then grow rapidly, and must be tied in an upright form to the portion of the stock left above the eye for that purpose. When it has made a good growth, and during the month of July or August, the stock should be cut off close to the shoot by a sloping back cut, when it will soon be covered with the growth of the wood. Those stocks that have not taken, should be grafted as soon in the Spring as that operation can be performed.

Preparation of Scions.—These are usually selected from the young wood of the previous season's growth, as well as those of one or even two years; though the former is to be preferred, and should be taken from the outside branches that have been fully exposed to the sun and air. They should be cut from the parent tree, any time from January to the period of growth. When they are collected, label each sort correctly, and place them in the ground, covered to within an inch of their tops, till the season of grafting arrives, which is just before the buds open to growth. Cut the scions into lengths of from three to five eyes; and where there is an abundance, use the middle portion of the shoot only.

Planting.—This season extends from the first of November till the swelling of the buds in Spring. Autumnal planting is to be preferred in light, dry soils; and Spring planting in retentive and heavy soils. Any time during the Winter season will do, when neither frost nor snow prevents the operation; but do not at any time expose the roots of trees in frosty, dry, windy weather; and in lifting trees, always retain as many of the fibres as practicable, and cut off neatly all that are bruised; with these precautions, trees from five to fifteen years old may be safely removed. We have seen entire orchards totally ruined at first by careless planting. In some, the trees lying to one side just as chance or the wind made them; in others, the trees hard-looking and bark-bound by deep planting. The former is sheer neglect in securing the tree to a stake; the latter, misapplied care. Writers on the subject say, "Dig a pit eighteen inches or two feet deep, and fill it up with rich compost; plant the tree therein one or two inches deeper than it was in the nursery row." This looks very well, but when applied it proves a grave to thousands. In the first place, the hole is much too deep: the soil, being all loose and fresh, decomposes, and falls down a few inches, taking the tree with it, so that in two years (just when the tree should put forth luxuriantly) it falls into the pit prepared for it, never to recover. Dig the pit or hole fully one foot deep, and three or four feet wide; break and prepare the soil well, in which place on its top your tree, over which lay a load of well prepared soil, sufficient to cover the roots entirely. Place a strong support to the tree, to prevent the wind disturbing the roots. The soil will settle, but not so as to take the roots of the tree into a tub of clay; they will always be on the surface, where nature intended them. As the tree will now rely on the new, vigorous fibres, which will be produced in its new station, if the soil be fine, moist, and warmed by the sun's influence, no fears need be entertained but that they will come forth to carry on the growth of the plant. Many trees have to be procured from a distance, perhaps thousands of miles. If nursery trees, they are generally *packed* in bundles,—packed is perhaps too business-like an expression,—they are *tied* like a bundle of fuel for the kitchen. Trees that have to be sent a great distance should be packed in boxes. The purchaser had better pay twice the cost of such, to have it done, as they are frequently as dry as rods when they come to hand. In such a case, have the trees soaked in water a few hours, and cover them up in wet straw or hay for twelve hours more; then puddle their roots in earth made to the consistency of thin mush. Plant them out in their proper places, and give the stems and branches a syringing with water every day till they have begun to grow, and occasionally afterwards. If you have not got a *syringe*, use a bowl, a basin, or any other utensil that will distribute the water.

ALMOND.

Amy'gdalus commūnis.—*Amandier*, Fr.—*Mandelbaum*, Ger.

THIS fruit is a native of China and other eastern countries. In the south of Europe it is cultivated to a great extent, for export, and several thousand tons are annually brought to this country. It could, however, be very readily cultivated in the latitudes and soils of Virginia and North Carolina. It is one of the fruits mentioned in the history of the Israelites, and was held in great esteem by the ancients. The tree is very similar to the Peach, in growth, blossom, and fruit; the flower, however, is much larger and more ornamental. The kernel (which is the only valuable part of the fruit) enters largely into confectionery of every kind. The toilet, too, is furnished with oils of various names extracted from it, such as Milk of Roses, Macassar Oil, Russia Oil, Kalydore, &c. There are several varieties of the fruit, but all known as Bitter and Sweet Almonds.

Sultane is a thin-shelled Sweet Almond; nut about an inch in length, firm, oval; shell light-colored, tender, and very porous; kernel rich and sweet.

Jordan or *Thick-Shelled.*—Size of the former; shell light-colored, smooth and porous; kernel rich and very sweet.

Amy'gdalis amara is the *Bitter Almond.* Fruit very similar to the others; shell hard; kernel bitter; used for condiments, and by wine-bibbers to allay the fumes of wine.

PROPAGATION AND CULTURE.—The Almond is propagated by

the kernel or seed, when the object is to obtain new varieties, in the same manner as the Peach. It can be perpetuated by budding, and is most permanent when grown upon the Plum stock; but in a dry, sandy soil, they will do best on their own stock. As a general rule, soil that grows the Peach will suit the Almond. See article Peach.

Gathering of the Fruit.—The fruit should be allowed to remain on the tree until the rind opens and becomes quite brown, and the kernels firm and solid, when it may be gathered and gradually dried till the shell becomes hard, after which it may be stored away for use.

APPLE.

Pyrus Mălus.—*Pomme*, Fr.—*Apfel*, Ger.

Of all the fruits cultivated in this country, the Apple is undoubtedly the most valuable. It is the fruit of the Peasant and the President, of the rich and the poor; and is suited to 346,500 square miles of the United States. At what period it became known is involved in obscurity. It is a native of several countries and peculiarly so of this; and the delightful odor of the Wild Crab of Virginia, when in bloom, is gratefully remembered by every traveler who passes that region in March and April. The tree is naturally long-lived; history asserts that it has been known to live "over a thousand years," though we would rather ascribe to it one-fourth of that period. There is no climate in the world where the Apple is brought to such perfection as in this. It can be had in perfection throughout the year, forming always an agreeable and luxurious addition to the food of man. The fruit, when ripe, is laxative; and when boiled or roasted it has been found serviceable in cases of weakness and indigestion, as also in putrid and malignant fevers.

The constitution of the Apple is adapted to every kind of soil. There are known to be about eight hundred varieties in cultivation, three-fourths of which are not worth attention, and of the remaining fourth, the following list contains all that are really excellent. We introduce to the notice of our readers such varieties only as have been tested and can be relied upon for a crop, comprising a succession from the earliest to the latest. Every person will understand our expressions of large, medium, small, round, flat, oval and long, when applied to the Apple, its size and character being so familiar to civilized man.

SUMMER APPLES. *Early Harvest*, *Prince's Harvest*, *Yellow Harvest*, &c.—This is the best early American Apple at present known, being a healthy growing tree, and a great bearer. *Fruit* of a pale yellow color, round form, medium size, skin waxy, smooth, with faint pale dots. Flesh tender and very juicy, of a sprightly, crisp flavor. Ripe early in July; fit for either dessert or cooking.

Striped Harvest.—A beautiful American variety, of excellent growth and very productive, takes the market well. *Fruit* under medium size, of a pale-yellow color, striped with red, profusely so next the sun, round form. Flesh very juicy and tender, of a superior flavor. A dessert fruit, ripe in July.

Bevan's Favorite.—An American fruit of great beauty; a constant bearer and of free growth. *Fruit* flat, greenish-yellow, highly colored with bright red, medium size. Flesh crisp, juicy, of a yellow-white color. Ripe from the middle to the end of July.

Bough, or *Large Yellow Bough*, is perhaps the finest looking fruit brought to our market, for which purpose we expressly notice it. We think it too large for the table, and it is not fit for the kitchen. *Fruit* large, oval, of a pale greenish-yellow. Flesh pure white, tender, sweet and crisp. Ripe in July and August.

Early Red Margaret, or *Red Juneating.*—An American

sort, of excellent qualities. *Fruit* medium size, of an oval form, pale green color, freely striped with dark red. Flesh yellow-white, of a very agreeable flavor, fit for the dessert or kitchen. Ripe in August.

Summer Pearmain, or *Autumn Pearmain* of some.—This is the very best fruit in its season, and has been long known in this vicinity. Tree of slender growth but well formed; a regular bearer. *Fruit* long oval, medium size, of a russety-yellow color, shaded with green and red. Flesh firm, brownish-yellow, crisp, juicy, and high flavored; suitable for the dessert or kitchen. Ripe in August and early September.

Maiden's Blush.—Supposed to be an American variety. Exceedingly beautiful; a great bearer, of good habit. *Fruit* medium size, flat; color pale yellow with a bright red cheek, or if grown in the shade, tinted with blush. Flesh white, tender, with a pleasant flavor. In use from August to October, and fit for either the table or kitchen.

Hawthornden.—A very popular Scotch Apple; a great and early bearer, fairly maintaining its character in this country; it is of dwarf growth and spreading form. *Fruit* very similar in size and shape to the former, though not so highly colored Flesh pure white, juicy, and mild flavored, suitable for either the table or cooking. Ripe from August to October.

FALL APPLES. *Rambo*, or *Red Seek-no-further*, is one of our most valuable varieties for the market, table, or kitchen, and is a native of this vicinity. *Fruit* about medium size, flat, with a smooth, yellow-white skin, marbled and speckled with rough red spots. Flesh yellowish-white, rich, and sprightly. In use from September to November.

Fall Pippin, or *Holland Pippin* of some.—Whoever has visited Philadelphia market in September and October has seen this Apple. *Fruit* large, round, of a fine, smooth, greenish yellow color, with an occasional blush. Flesh white, mellow, spicy, rich and tender. Very popular for either the dessert or kitchen.

White Seek-no-further.—A very popular variety; trees of free growth and good bearing. *Fruit* round, rather tapering towards the eye, of a yellowish-white color; skin smooth, with russety spots. Flesh yellow, rich, juicy and tender. A table fruit of great excellence; in use from September to November.

Bell-flower, or *Yellow Bell-flower* of some, is everywhere esteemed for its many good qualities. It is one of the most prolific bearers, and, being a native, well adapted for general culture. *Fruit* very large, of a conical form; color creamy-yellow, with a few brown spots. Flesh tender, juicy, crisp, with a sprightly flavor, having a large core. Fit for the table or kitchen. In use from September to December.

Autumn Pearmain, or *Winter Pearmain.*—This variety is not excelled by any of our Fall or Winter fruits. Wood of slender growth, but producing great crops. *Fruit* oblong, medium size, of a yellowish color, stained and mottled with a brownish-red. Flesh pale lemon-yellow, tender, with an agreeable, aromatic flavor. Fit for dessert or cooking. Ripe in October to January.

WINTER APPLES. *Cumberland Spice*, or *White Bell-flower* of some, is a general favorite, producing great crops. *Fruit* oblong, large size, tapering towards the eye; of a yellowish-white color, marked with a few reddish-brown dots, having a large core. Flesh white, very juicy, tender, with a delicately agreeable flavor. In use from October to February.

Bullock's Pippin, or *Sheep-Nose.*—This is a productive variety, universally cultivated for its luscious flavor. *Fruit* conical, of a yellow russety color, footstalk long. Flesh yellow, very tender, mild, rich, and juicy. An American sort, in eating from October to January. It is called by Eastern growers "*Golden Russet*," confounding it with the well-known old Apple of that name, to which it has no affinity.

Wine Apple, or *Hay's Apple.*—Well known in this vicinity as a superb Winter fruit, of large size; of a round, flattened form, skin yellow, nearly covered with bright red. Flesh yellowish-white, crisp, and juicy, with a vinous and pleasant flavor. A table and kitchen fruit, in use from October to January.

Rhode Island Greening.—A favorite fruit, extensively cultivated, and produces immense crops in almost every variety of soil. *Fruit* large, round, very regular form, with a smooth, dark green skin. Flesh yellow, close, sprightly, with a slightly aromatic flavor. In use for the kitchen or table from October to January.

Roman Stem —A great favorite in New Jersey, where it is very productive, forming a very handsome, round-headed tree. *Fruit* round, medium size, of a pale yellow color, with a few reddish specks. Flesh delicate, with a rich, juicy, agreeable flavor. Ripe from November to March, and fit for either the table or cooking.

Æsopus Spitzenburg.—There is perhaps not a fruit in the whole catalogue more beautiful to look upon than this variety, and it is second to none in quality. *Fruit* large, partially oblong; skin smooth, of a yellowish-green, and nearly covered with brilliant red. Flesh yellow, crisp and juicy, of a rich flavor, with a large core. Ripe in November to January.

Monmouth Pippin.—I have not seen an Apple for many years that so much riveted my attention as this, at the Exhibition of the New Jersey Horticultural Society, in 1846. The tree is of excellent habit, and a good bearer. *Fruit* over medium size, roundish, flat; smooth, russety-green skin, marked with dots of brown. Flesh firm, yellow-white, crisp, juicy and high flavored. In use from November to March. Fit for the dessert or the kitchen.

Baldwin.—A celebrated Apple of the Eastern States, where the tree is reputed to be a great bearer, and cultivated extensively for the market, sending us a supply every season. *Fruit* round, rather conical, of a yellow ground, covered with crimson and red, having a few russet spots and streaks Flesh yellow, crisp, and of a peculiarly rich flavor. Ripe from November to February. An excellent table fruit.

Newton Pippin.—There are two varieties of this prince of fruits, the Yellow and the Green, differing in color, very much alike in form, though the Yellow appears to be a little flatter than the Green. *Fruit* medium size, round, obscurely ribbed towards the eye, of a dull yellow-green, with a brownish blush on one side, slightly covered with brown dots. Flesh firm, yellowish-white, very crisp, juicy, having an exceedingly peculiar rich flavor. For eating or cooking it has as yet no equal. In use from November to May, retaining all its aroma till the last. A native of Long Island, where the original tree, I believe, still exists. It requires a rich, loamy soil.

Lady Apple.—A very popular variety, introduced from France, and is generally cultivated as a leading Winter fruit which it produces in clusters. The tree is of an elegant, upright, strong growth. *Fruit* small, regularly round, though rather flattened; color bright yellow, with a lively dark red cheek. Flesh white, tender, juicy and crisp. A valuable market variety, in use from December to April.

Tewksbury Winter Blush.—A handsome American fruit, not equalled for long keeping by any other sort. A great bearer and of good growth. *Fruit* of medium size, round, flat form; skin smooth, yellow, with a bright red cheek. Flesh yellowish-white, juicy, and well flavored. In use from January to July.

CIDER APPLES. *Winesap* is a great bearer, grows freely though rather straggling, and is extensively grown in the sandy soils of New Jersey. *Fruit* medium size, roundish, yellow, almost entirely covered with dull red. Flesh yellow, firm, crisp, juicy, and high flavored. A Winter fruit.

Harrison.—A handsome growing tree of New Jersey, of the very highest character as a Cider Apple, producing large crops. *Fruit* medium size, round-oval; yellow, with rough, black specks. Flesh yellow, rich flavor. Ripe in November.

Hagloe Crab.—A celebrated fruit for early use, either for cider or the kitchen. It is a strong grower and an abundant bearer. *Fruit* medium size, flat, greenish-yellow streaked with red. Flesh soft, juicy, with a rich flavor. Ripe in August and September.

Siberian Crab.—This variety is cultivated exclusively for preserving, being very small, with a clear, waxy skin, either Yellow or Red, there being two varieties. The Red makes a very ornamental tree when loaded with its brilliant fruit, being like so many pendant garnets.

CULTURE.—The best soil for the Apple is that of a loamy, friable nature, avoiding sand and clay, in either of which this tree is short-lived. The finest trees and orchards are planted on a deep, sandy loam, either on a dry bottom or having a good descent for carrying off the water. It is not our purpose to go into an elaborate detail of the management of an orchard; that would only confuse and mystify; our aim is to state only what is essential, and to do it with brevity and precision There is no country that possesses greater advantages of climate for fruit culture than the United States; yet, as we have stated, we see fine young trees left to the mercy of the elements without any support; we see no disposition to arrange or form the head; no hand to thin out the crops; all, all is left to nature; even the soil has no annual or tri-annual material given to keep it in a state to yield a regular and continued crop. The trees, in consequence, get distorted, the limbs broken down with their harvest to their lazy lords; and then commences the "besom of destruction," to annihilate their existence, with saw and axe to cut off their broken branches; disease takes hold of the tree, and it comes to a premature old age, having not lived half its days. Such has been the fate of many an orchard, and such is the treatment most frequently pursued in the present day. The first object of attention in planting an orchard, ought to be to have the ground well ploughed, deep—

even trench-ploughed. Manure heavily, put on a Potato or Corn crop the year previous to planting out, and cultivate it freely the whole season. The soil will then be in order to receive the trees. Plant them from forty to fifty feet apart, giving the tree at once a strong support, to prevent its being tossed with the winds. Tie between the tree and the stake some soft material, which will keep the bark from being chafed. Experience teaches that all young orchards should be cultivated and cropped with any kind of grain or root crops excepting grass or hay. After the trees have come into a good bearing state, grass is not at all objectionable; but as soon as the trees show any indications of a meagre and stunted growth, the ground should be well enriched in the vicinity of their roots. We see no reason why fruit trees should not occupy the space allowed for brush and saplings around the fields and about the fences. It cannot be the cost, for that is a mere trifle. Every farmer may at least grow a part, and should have a few reserve trees by him every year. It is merely because it is customary to allow these "weeds of the forest" to grow in place of luscious fruit.

Pruning.—This object is generally considered a labor, instead of a pleasant pastime. We can never admit that it is necessary to use an axe and a saw to prune a tree, more especially a fruit tree; that treatment belongs to the dark ages. A strong pruning-knife, good hands, with a judicious head, are the accompaniments of the orchardist. Cut off all cross branches, shorten those that stretch out beyond the general outline of the tree; thin out all superabundant wood, to allow the permanent branches and shoots to be from six to twelve inches apart. It will rarely be necessary to cut off a shoot of one inch in diameter.

Insects.—We are not aware of any destructive enemy to the Apple tree that cannot be kept under by a moderate share of vigilance. The *Borer*, a white, fleshy grub that commits

its depredations just at the surface of the ground, perforating every part of the stem, is the greatest enemy. Heaping round the tree, during the month of May, about eight inches of coal ashes, lime, or sand, will greatly prevent it. These heaps must be spread down again in October or November. It is said that by putting a peck of hot lime about the stem of a tree that is affected by this grub, it will be entirely restored. Naturalists say that this insect (*Sapènda bivittàta*) remains two or three years in the tree, and comes out in a butterfly form in June, flying about at night and depositing its eggs on the tree close to the surface of the ground.

Caterpillars may be kept under (and in fact it is the only way to do it) by destroying their nests early in the morning, or about noon. If they are allowed to progress, they will soon cover an orchard; while, when taken in time, they are very readily destroyed.

Gathering the Fruit.—Hand-picking is undoubtedly the best way of collecting the fruit, and whether for family use or the market, the superior quality and appearance of such will command a price that will more than cover the expense. Early fruits should be handled very carefully. Winter fruits may remain on the tree till the approach of frost, when they should be collected, and those for sale put into good barrels at once, to be conveyed to market when required. Those intended for family use should be placed in a dry shed for two weeks, and then carefully wiped with a cloth, and put away in a dry cellar, free from frost. Those that are required to keep till May and June should be packed in dry sand, or some other material, to exclude them from the air.

THE APRICOT.

Prúnus armenìca.—Abricotier, Fr.—*Aprikosenbaum*, Ger.

The Apricot is one of the most beautiful of fruits, and has been cultivated for about eighteen hundred years. It is a native of China and Japan, growing in great abundance on the dry mountains of those countries. Some travelers also mention of its being found in Egypt. The fruit is much esteemed for making marmalades, jellies, and preserves. In its plain state it is considered wholesome and strengthening. In Europe it attains to very great perfection, though with us it never appears to grow to that size we have so frequently seen it there. A Moorpark Apricot, twelve inches in circumference, is a very imposing fruit, compared with the nut-like productions usually seen in our markets. It ripens at a very desirable period of the season, between the period of the late Cherries and early Peaches. We introduce the following as the best sorts:

Breda.—A small fruit, about four inches in circumference, very abundant, round form, deep brown-orange color, with a few blush spots towards the sun. Flesh deep orange, separating from the stone; flavor good, kernel sweet, which is a dis tinguishing character in this variety.

Hemskirke.—*Fruit* medium size (two inches diameter), of a round form, color bright orange. Flesh dark orange; flavor very juicy and rich. Tree of vigorous growth and an abundant bearer.

Moorpark.—It is admitted that this variety is the best of the family, and is universally cultivated. I have seen a tree of this sort that covered a wall sixteen feet high and one hundred feet long. Its growth in this climate is not so free as the former, but it is a greater bearer, and always produces a crop. Size, the largest from two to four inches in diameter; color pale yellow; form round-oval; flesh bright orange; separating freely from the stone; flavor very rich. Growth strong; eyes close; foliage large. Delights in a deep, sandy loam. Ripe about the middle of July. The whole of this class of fruits ripen in this month, with us; but if picked before being fully ripe and put into an ice-house they will be in eating two weeks longer.

Peach Apricot or *Abricot peche*, of the French.—There is very little difference between this variety and the former; indeed it is so trifling that very few could detect it. It possesses the same characters and ripens at the same time, but the wood has not the eyes so closely set on it, nor is the foliage so heart-shaped. One grand essential to the production of fine Apricots is to thin out the fruit well, not allowing it to remain within two or three inches of each other. There are about ten other varieties of the Apricot, but all inferior, so far as has been tested by us, to those now described.

Culture.—This tree rarely succeeds well in this country unless protected by a wall or fence ; not that it does not grow as a standard, like other fruit trees, but in that position it rarely matures a crop, except in city gardens, the early Spring frosts destroying the blossoms. It should be placed on an east, west, or north aspect, avoiding a south. It requires a good, rich, sandy, loamy soil. The Curculio appears to be particularly fond of the fruit.

Pruning may be entirely dispensed with after the tree is formed, merely keeping the branches within bounds, and training the shoots in any required direction. As a standard, in city gardens, it is both useful and ornamental, being the first tree in bloom of the season, having a large, shining, green foliage, and generally producing a good crop.

Propagation.—It is too frequently budded on the Peach stock by nurserymen. On such it is short-lived, not constitutionally so, but the stock on which it depends for life fails in a few years, unless the Borer be prevented from attacking it. The best, and indeed the only stock that should be used, is the Plum, on which it should be budded in July or August, and on it will grow half a century. Very good fruit can be raised by planting the stones, in the same manner as the Peach.

CHERRY.

Cerasus, var.—*Cerisier*, Fr.—*Kirschenbaum*, Ger.

SOME species of the Cherry is native to every temperate climate. History records its culture before the Christian era. It is the earliest of our stone fruits, and comes into use about the 8th or 20th of June, according to the season. The tree is of great diversity of habit, size and shape. The fruit, too, possesses every variety of flavor, from the most tart to a honey sweet. In cookery and distillation it is compounded into endless forms. In ancient and modern times it is peculiarly a wayside tree—an avenue of Cherry trees characterizing the dwellings of the great in the 16th century. The medicinal properties of the fruit are rather vague, though it is considered wholesome. Its gum is supposed to be nearly equal to the gum arabic of commerce. The wood is extensively used in domestic cabinet work. There are nearly a hundred varieties, whose qualities may all be embraced in half a dozen sorts.

Bigarreau.—Color pale yellow, with red cheek, and when fully ripe, of a bright amber; large size, irregularly heart-shaped. Flesh firm, adhering to the stone; rich and high flavored. Stalk about two inches long; growth strong and upright. A great bearer; hangs long on the tree. Ripe about the 4th of July.

Black Tartarian, or *Black Circassian.*—*Fruit* very large; irregularly heart-shaped; of a shining black color when fully ripe; stalk an inch and a half long. Flesh dark purple, very rich and juicy; stone quite small. Ripe from the 20th to the end of June. The finest Black Cherry that is grown. A handsome tree, of rapid growth and large foliage.

Carnation.—Color a bright, shining, waxy, marbled red; fine round form; stalk short and stout. Flesh tender when fully ripe, of a rich sub-acid flavor. One of the best cooking varieties. Ripe about the first of July, and hangs long on the tree; a good bearer. Tree low-growing and round-headed.

Elton.—Color pale, waxy yellow, cheek next the sun of a shining, pale red, mottled, or streaked. The very largest size, heart-shaped; stalk one and a half to two inches long. Flesh, when fully ripe, tender, juicy and of the very best flavor. Ripe about the 20th of June. Tree of strong growth and regular form, foliage large.

Kentish.—There are several varieties that go under this name, such as May Cherry, Early Richmond, Flemish of some. There is also a Late Kentish, or Pie Cherry, very common. The sort we now allude to is the *Early Kentish*, or *Early Richmond.* It generally produces its fruit in pairs, of a fine dark red color when ripe. Stalk about an inch long, adhering to the stone. Flesh juicy, of a rather sharp, acid flavor. Ripe from the 15th to 25th of June. A low, spreading tree, in very general cultivation.

Late Duke.—Color dark red; large size; of a heart shape, rather rounding. Flesh amber colored, rich and juicy. Stone large, oval. Ripe, end of July. Does well in light soils. An excellent late variety, either for the dessert or the kitchen.

May Duke.—Every lover of this fruit has heard of the May Duke Cherry, which for fine flavor, prolific bearing, and early ripeness, stands alone. When fully ripe it is "*the Cherry*," and should be in every garden or orchard. Color very dark red, round form. Flesh very juicy, rich and melting; stone small; a great bearer; tree regularly formed, wood short and full of spurs. Ripe about the 8th of June. This variety is invariably pulled before it is ripe.

Morello.—The latest of all the Cherries. It hung on the tree with us, last year, till the 24th of August. They are so tart that neither birds nor bipeds partake. *Fruit* round; color very dark, or quite black when fully ripe. Flesh very dark, more juicy than any other variety, and has not an equal for the kitchen. It is in use from the middle of July to the middle of August. Tree of medium growth, round and pendulous form. The Common Morello is a smaller and inferior variety.

White Bigarreau, White Heart, and *Oxheart* of some.—It is not our purpose to decide what fruits belong to these names, whereof so many writers disagree. Our object is to call attention to the variety that ripens about the 15th of June, just between the May Duke and the Elton. We cultivate it under the former name. *Fruit* heart-shaped, of a pale yellowish-white color, with a marbled-red on the side towards the sun. Flesh, when fully ripe, tender and luscious; stone large. Tree regularly formed, and a great bearer when fully established.

These constitute the best of the Cherries, and such as produce their fruit throughout the season. I am aware of the very high character borne by some of the new sorts, which we have not tested, nor have they been fully tried by others. To enter into a detail of such, would frustrate our object, in directing attention only to the best known for family use or the market.

Culture.—A light, sandy loam, in an open exposure, is the best soil for the Cherry. Though we have them bearing fruit in both wet and dry soils, yet the finest orchards are known to be on a rich, sandy loam, over a gravelly bottom. We prefer planting this tree early in Spring; they will require to be twenty-five feet apart. The pruning is of the simplest form, many of the kind rarely requiring the knife, while others, as the Bigarreau, need to have the long, rampant shoots that stretch beyond the boundary of the tree shortened every September, till they are formed.

Propagation.—This is done both by budding and grafting. The former is the most general practice of nurserymen, who sow yearly, in August, large quantities of the Common Black Cherry, about one inch deep, which vegetate freely in Spring, and after two years growth are fit to be budded. This is done in August or even the first of September, according to the weather. Transplant the stocks one year before they are worked; they thus make more fibrous roots, and when required to be moved again will grow with greater certainty.

The Cherry is brought to our markets in the most slovenly state, in large tubs, and frequently pulled from the stems, a mere compound of half-bruised, half-rotten, and half-ripe fruit, and of course it brings much less than its real value. Cherries should be pulled with care, having the stems all attached to the fruit, and handled as little as possible. If for the table, pick them a few hours before they are wanted, and put them in a cool place. If for the market, put them in shallow vessels to prevent bruising as much as possible. They will bring double the price of fruit in the ordinary state.

CURRANT.

Rìbes rùbrum.—*Groseille à grappes d'outre*, Fr.—*Johannisbure*, Ger.

THE Red and Black Currant of the gardens are considered natives of the northern parts of Europe. The Black is evidently an inhabitant of a cool climate, for it rarely produces its fruit in perfection, the berries falling before being ripe. There are several varieties of Currants natives of North America, but very different in habit and character from those cultivated. There are few or no medicinal virtues attached to the fruit. "Currant Wine" is a beverage that was known to our fathers, but has been superseded by the more expensive and fashionable "Port and Madeira." The fruit has a pleasant, cooling, acid flavor, relished by most individuals when ripe. From it there is a very excellent jelly made, an indispensable condiment to many fashionable dishes of the day. The green fruit is also used for tarts, but for that purpose is much inferior to Rhubarb and Gooseberries.

Ribes nigra, or the *Black Currant*, is a very rich fruit, produced in bunches of from three to five inches long, but requires a moist, cool situation, shaded from the noon-day sun. There are several varieties of it, called *Black Grape*, *Black Naples*, and the *Common Black*. The fruit is made into jelly or jam, and much used in consumptive complaints.

The *Red Currant* is a very familiar fruit, susceptible of great improvement by culture, worthy of the best care, and generally gets none. There are several varieties of it, at least it is grown under a variety of names. I have cultivated *New Red*, *Knight's Early Red*, *Red Grape*, and lastly, *May's Victoria*, neither of which excel the old *Red Dutch* that I cultivated twenty-five years ago. Red Currants and Raspberries make the finest jelly.

Champagne.—This is a variety evidently between the Red and White, of a pink color.

White Dutch.—The White Currant is preferred for the table, it being more sweet and palatable than any of the other sorts. It grows like the two preceding, and requires the same treatment.

Propagation and Culture.—The best mode of increasing this plant is by selecting cuttings of good, strong, young wood, about a foot long. The eyes from the lower part of the shoot, for about eight inches, must be cut out previous to planting, which will prevent suckers being thrown up from the roots. Plant them as early in Spring as the ground can be prepared, or late in the Autumn, just before the ground is closed with the frost. A partially shaded situation is most suitable, though they will do in any rich, moist ground; in two years they will make fine plants, when they must be removed to where they are intended to remain for fruiting, (suckers and layers should never be used). Their after-culture is merely to train up the plant to one stem, about a foot high, then allow it to spread and ramify uniformly, but never admit it to sucker from the root.

Pruning.—Thin out the shoots to allow all to stand free and clear of each other, then shorten back the young wood from about three to six inches of the preceding year's growth. This makes the bushes *spur*, as gardeners term it, and on these spurs the fruit is produced. The plant must be yearly supplied with manure among their roots, digging the ground carefully every Spring or Fall. By this treatment the fruit will be like bunches of Grapes, and form a great contrast to the meagre affairs so generally seen in our markets. Even in our best gardens their culture is very imperfectly attended to, producing fruit all skin and seeds, and giving a very faint idea of the richness and perfection to which it can attain. Plant them cight feet apart, and if well treated they will last twenty years.

FIG.

Ficus Cárica.—Figuier, Fr.—*Feigenbaum*, Ger.

The Fig is one of the fruits first mentioned in history. Its cultivation appears to have been coeval with that of the Apple and the Grape. It has been admitted through all ages as an article of food, and some nations have been so exceedingly fond of the fruit that its exportation was forbidden. If history is to be relied on, we are retrograding in the culture and improvement of the Fig. Pliny, the Roman naturalist, is said to have accurately described about thirty sorts. It was extensively used in all ceremonies, and was presented to appease anger. Asia is its native country, and we read of specimens of the fruit having been brought from the "Land of Canaan." It is cultivated to an immense extent in the south of Europe, and dried and exported. Many thousand tons reach this country that might be grown with great facility along our [illegible], from North Carolina to Florida. It is not hardy enough to stand our Winters without protection; but south of Virginia it might be made an article of profit, independent of its healthful influence on the constitution. There are supposed to be about forty varieties, though we might very readily class them into the White, Black, and Brown.

Black Ischia, about two inches long and two inches in diameter, rather flat towards the apex; deep purple color. Flesh red, of excellent flavor, and very productive. They all ripen in July, August, and September; and again a small crop in April and May.

Brown Turkey.—In general culture. Size smaller than the former; color brown; a great bearer. Flesh pale red.

White Marseilles, White Celestial, &c.—Fruit pale yellowish-white; round form; medium size. Flesh rose-white, very high flavored; a great bearer.

Propagation.—The Fig is increased by cuttings and layers of the preceding year's wood, which root readily in moist, sandy soil. Cuttings of about a foot in length, planted any time from November to February, in a shaded, moist, soil, will root the first season, when they may be planted into a situation appropriated for them. Layers are made by taking a branch of two to three feet long, making an incision in it nearly half way through the shoot, entering the knife half an inch below an eye and drawing it towards the point of the shoot about two inches, which will form what gardeners call a tongue, on the lower extremity of which is the eye; bend this portion gently, placing it under the ground about four inches, where it will form roots in a few months. Early the following Spring these layers may be taken off and planted where they are required.

Culture.—The Fig is not very particular in regard to soils. We have seen it covering an extent of forty feet by twenty, in all kinds of soils, from sand to clay; but the fairest fruit is obtained from trees grown on a sandy, loamy soil, with a dry bottom. On very rich soils it grows too much to wood, on very poor soils the fruit ripens prematurely. *Fig orchards* should be planted about twenty feet apart, and cultivated between the trees, till they nearly cover the ground. Never speak of your figs blooming: they never flower, to the eye; and the mode of fructifying is rather a speculation, even in the present day. "There is something very singular in the fructification of the Fig: it has no visible flower, for the fruit arises immediately from the joints of the tree, in the form of little buds, with a perforation at the end, but not opening or showing anything like petals or the ordinary parts of fructification. As the Fig enlarges, the flower comes to maturity in concealment, and in eastern countries the fruit is improved by a singular operation called *caprification*. This is performed by suspending by threads, above the cultivated figs, branches of the wild fig, which are full of a species of cynips. When the insect has become winged, it quits the wild Fig and penetrates the cultivated ones, for the purpose of laying its eggs; and thus it appears both to insure the fructification by dispersing the pollen, and afterwards to hasten the ripening by puncturing the pulp and causing a change of the nutricious juices. In France this operation is imitated by inserting straws dipped in olive oil."—*Lib. of Ent. Knowledge.*

PRUNING.—"The more you prune the less the crop," is proverbial in Fig culture. All that is required is to shorten any irregular or overgrowing shoot, and cut out dead wood, of which more or less will show itself every few years.

FILBERT.

Córylus Avellána.—*Noisette*, Fr.—*Nussbaum*, Ger.

THE common Hazel Nut will never be an article of profit to the American gardener or husbandman; yet we introduce the subject for some who cultivate for pleasure, variety, and amusement. It is a curious fact that all good things come 'from the east:" so say writers on the Filbert. It comes from *Pontus.* Thousands grow wild on the "braes" of Scotland, and millions are over the whole United States, from Maine to Texas. Cultivation has greatly improved the size, but we doubt of the flavor being more delicious. In its wild state it is a large-sized shrub, with a gray colored bark, and roundish, heart-shaped leaves. The male catkins (flowers) appear on the preceding year's shoots, in Autumn, and wait all Winter for the expansion of the female flowers in Spring. The varieties in quality are all very similar, though they considerably differ in appearance. The *Red*, *White*, *Cosford*, and *Frizzled*, are sufficient for cultivation.

Propagation.—By layers, as directed for Figs; by suckers, which spring up *freely* from the roots; or by seeds, that may be purchased at the fruit-stores, in any of our cities.

Culture.—They like a heavy, moist loam, and will grow where partially shaded. Plant them eight or ten feet apart. Prune as directed for currants, merely to check the superabundant growth, to throw them into spur-buds, for fruiting.

GOOSEBERRY.

Rìbes Grossulària.—*Groseille à Maquereau*, Fr.—*Stachelbeerstrauch*, Ger.

This fruit, so extensively cultivated in Britain, and also in some parts of this country, is not at all adapted to a southern climate. It is only occasionally that a crop is attained here, even with the best of care. It requires a cool climate, or some local cause, to attain the perfection for which it is so justly celebrated. It is a native of this country and Europe. We have seen it wild on the Alleghany mountains; and before we see it perfect in culture, we must re-produce from our native sorts. It is highly esteemed in culinary purposes for tarts and preserves; and when fully ripe is laxative, and considered a very wholesome dessert fruit. The finest crops we have seen in this country were grown in the vicinity of Montreal and the Lakes, and near Pittsburg, between the Alleghany and Monongahela rivers, over which the smoke of that city of iron continually rolls, during June, July, and August, which entirely prevents the mildew, the only enemy to the culture of this fruit in this quarter. There are a thousand varieties of it, which may be detailed in *Reds*, *Whites*, *Yellows* and *Greens*, all fancifully named, according to the ideas of the growers. They ripen from the middle to the end of July.

Propagation.—The method is precisely as detailed for Currants, both in culture and pruning. In warm seasons, just after rain, some sorts are frequently attacked with mildew, which baffles our skill to prevent, though we may retard its progress by showering them with sulphur-water. The cure, however, is nearly as bad as the disease. Mildew makes its appearance about the middle of June, in the form of brownish-white spots on the fruit. As soon as observed, the berries may at once be pulled for the kitchen or market, for they never get over it, and the longer they hang the worse they become. It is not soil that is the cause, for we have had them some seasons all destroyed, while last year the same plants, in the same ground, were as fine as they could be, in size, form, and flavor. It is an atmospheric disease, and only that. The fruit is in size from half an inch to two inches in diameter; the medium sized are the best flavored. The very largest have been known to weigh an ounce and a half; but they are uniformly of inferior quality. For flavor none excel the following:

Reds.	*Yellows.*
Red Warrington,	Golden Yellow,
Champagne,	Early Sulphur,
Roaring Lion,	Yellow Ball,
Rough Red,	Golden Hero,
Red Jam,	Ashton Yellow,
Lancashire Lad.	Viper.

Whites.	*Greens.*
Queen of Sheba,	Gregory's Perfection,
White Eagle,	Green Ocean,
Venus,	Green Laurel,
White Smith,	Green Gage,
White Sulphur,	Jolly Angler,
Hedgehog.	Green Gascoigne.

GRAPE.

Vitis, var.—*Vigne*, Fr.—*Weintrauben*, Ger.

The culture of the vine is spoken of in the remotest ages. The antediluvians were no doubt perfectly familiar with its growth and manufacture into an intoxicating drink. Providence, with a bountiful hand, distributes copiously over the earth those fruits which are for the comfort and luxury of man, who frequently converts these blessings into a curse, manufacturing with his own hands an engine for his destruction. The practice of not allowing vines to mature their fruit till the fourth year, was inculcated by Moses, who lectured on the subject to the Israelites. The Egyptians ascribed the manufacture of wine to Osiris, and the Grecians to Bacchus, whom, for the discovery, they elevated to the rank of a deity. Pliny describes many kinds of grapes, one shaped like a finger, which appears to be lost. They had a vine at that period, near Rome that annually produced about three barrels of pure juice. In those days, young men under thirty, and women, all their lifetime, were forbidden to drink wine. How would these regulations suit the moderns? Plato loved wine: he says, "Nothing more excellent or valuable than wine was ever granted by God to man." Ignatius Marennius killed his wife with a billet of wood, having caught her drinking wine. He was tried, and was acquitted of murder; but history does not say whether it was by his gold or a justification in the circumstances that he obtained his freedom. Cato records that the custom of kinsfolk kissing women when they met, was to know by their breath if they had been drinking wine! There is no fruit so wholesome—none so generally palatable—none that can be so universally cultivated—and none so remunerating as the Grape. Its rapidity of growth, productiveness, long life and simplicity of culture, may enable every farmer, at least, to live literally under his own vine. There is not a farmer or planter from New York to New Orleans but may cultivate, with a very small outlay, an abundance of this fruit. I never see long, naked post-rail fences, but am reminded of the neglect of this fruit: not that it does not deserve the very best of ground, the most studied culture; but here is a waste of land and the very support that would produce thousands of tons of this inestimable fruit. The extent of its culture in Ohio and other States is rapidly increasing. N. Longworth, Esq., of Cincinnati, a zealous horticulturist, has one hundred acres under culture, which he rents out to Swiss and German vine-dressers, who therefrom have an excellent living, and make him a bountiful return. The fruit is manufactured into wine, and sold at from 75 cents to $1.50 per gallon, and the produce of that vicinity is about six hundred barrels. This is merely "a drop in the bucket," compared with the immense import of the past year.* For this purpose their standard Grape is the Catawba,

* After deducting the export, there remains for home consumption 3,105,166 gallons, at a cost of $1,131,038.

and other native Grapes, of which the following are the best. If our own advice could prevail, we would plant only Isabella and Catawba, or improved varieties therefrom.

Bland or *Powell.*—Color pale red; fruit round; bunches short, with two or three shoulders when well-grown. Flesh pulpy, with a half sweet, subacid flavor, and a little of the peculiar musky tinge, characteristic of the Fox Grape. Foliage pale green underneath, and more rounding than any of the following sorts.

Catawba.—One of the best native Grapes; bunches rather regularly formed, with a few shoulders. Fruit round, of a bright red or coppery color when ripe. Flesh pulpy; rather juicy, and sweet when fully ripe, with a musky flavor. Foliage pale green, with a white down underneath, and more reflexed than that of the Isabella, which it very much resembles. This variety is most esteemed for wine, and when fully ripe, in my estimation, is the best of our native grapes for the table, though I cannot go so far as to say "it is luscious and high-flavored."

Elsingborough, Elsenborough, Elsinburg.—This Grape is a native of the sandy soils of New Jersey, where it is considered the best of the American Grapes. Bunches small, compact and shouldered; berries small, jet black, round, with a thin skin. Flesh without pulp, sweet and well-flavored. Foliage coarse, deeply five-lobed. Wood slender, very hardy.

Isabella.—This variety is hardier than either of the former, and may be cultivated as far north as the St. Lawrence. Bunches long, tapering, with very few shoulders. Berries oval, jet black, with a fine bloom. Skin thick. Flesh a little pulpy, very sweet, with a little touch of the musky flavor. Ripe about the end of September, but improves by hanging on the vines till frost. I have repeatedly handed ripe fruit of this Grape, with that of the Black Hamburg, to individuals entirely unacquainted with the flavor of grapes, and they have generally pronounced the Isabella the best and sweetest Grape.

Foliage large, three-lobed, with a white down underneath. Wood very strong, of a brownish-red color.

Ohio, or the *Segar-Box Grape*.—This variety was brought into notice by Mr. Longworth, of Cincinnati. Its history is rather obscure, though there is no doubt of its being a native It approaches nearer the Elsinburg than any other we cultivate, but is not so hardy as that sort. Bunches long, compact, and tapering, with one or two shoulders. *Berries* small, round, and jet black, with a thin skin. Flesh sweet and well flavored; the seeds large. Wood strong, shorter jointed than either the Isabella or Catawba, and requires to be laid in thin, or the fruit rots off before ripening. The plant is rather tender for us, being severely injured with me last Winter. All our native Grapes ripen from the 1st of September to the 1st of October; but I have found the flavor greatly improved by hanging on the vine as long as possible, keeping clear of frost. There are few bunches that will weigh one pound.

Propagation of the native Grape is a very simple process. They will all grow assuredly from layers of the preceding year's wood, or even of the wood of the current year. All that is required is merely to bend a shoot to the ground, make a hole four inches deep, and place the bend of the shoot in it. Cover it up firmly with the earth; give it frequent waterings in dry weather. In the month of November it will be fit to cut from the parent to plant in the vineyard, or in any other required locality. When it is planted out, cut it down to about two eyes from the ground; allow one of these only to grow the following season. It is also propagated by cuttings very generally, though there are some sorts rather shy to root by this method. We also grow them from eyes, as directed for foreign vines. *Grafting* can also be accomplished on the vine. Allow the stock to grow till it has made a leaf or two, then take a scion that has been retarded in a cool place, and prepare it either for whip or wedge grafting.

By Cuttings.—Shoots of last season's wood, cut into lengths of about a foot long (of many of the sorts), and planted into any rich, light soil, nearly their whole depth, will root in one season, and by care and pruning they will grow to fine plants in two years; when they should be planted out where they are intended to remain.

Soil.—The native vine will grow in any kind of soil, except that of a wet or clayey nature, and on any exposure and situation, except low valleys, where in some seasons it mildews and drops its fruit. The best soil is a rich and friable loam, under which there is a stony, sandy, or gravelly bottom. They do not require excessively rich soils, but they stand in need of semi-annual dressings with manures or rich composts, and if this is withheld they will deteriorate in quality and quantity The soil must be properly ameliorated and enriched before planting, and if trenched with the spade or plough, the benefit derived will amply repay the cost. For vineyards, plant them six feet apart, and eight feet from row to row; train them to trellises or poles made of Red Cedar wood, or White Oak. Eight feet in height for field culture will be sufficient; but for city gardens, where borders of rich soil are prepared for them, they will grow to any height, even to the roof of a five story dwelling, and there produce excessive crops. Trellises for training may be made of any shape or form, but those that are upright are preferable.

Pruning.—On the proper execution of this operation greatly depends the prosperity and fruitfulness of the vine. There is frequently so great a mystery thrown around these simple attentions that the timid are afraid even to touch the vine with the knife; while others, whose boldness goes farther than their knowledge, cut right and left with considerable dexterity, feeling satisfied if they show that the wood is at least cut off. To cut the shoots from three to ten eyes of the preceding year's wood, according to its strength, is a good general rule. To put our ideas in a tangible form, we will begin with the young plant. As above stated, cut it to within two eyes from the ground, from which allow one shoot to grow for the first season, and now call it a plant one year old; if the soil is in good order it will be fifteen feet long. In November, or before February, cut that shoot to about two feet from the ground, and allow three shoots to grow. They will each attain fifteen to twenty feet. It is now two years old. About the same period of the season lay the two lowest of these shoots horizontally and cut them to about twenty inches from the main stem; the most upright, cut at about two feet from the stem and allow the plant to make fruit this (the third) year. Six bunches will be quite enough. The plant being now formed, and having made, in the fourth season, a quantity of branches all covered with fruit, it is advisable to take only one bunch off each, and never take more than two. Leading branches will be required for the future plant. These may extend to fill up any given space, but all others must be topped two eyes beyond the fruit; that is, leave on two leaves nearer the extremity of the shoot than the bunches hang. This topping should be performed early in June, and when they make fresh shoots top them again and again. The leading shoots must also be topped as soon as they are at their required length. Where vines are needed to cover high arbors, or reach the top of dwellings, the shoots in the first and second year may be left from six to ten feet long.

Summer Pruning is generally very injudiciously performed. The vines are allowed to grow in every form till July or August, when they are thinned out and deprived of a great deal of young wood and foliage, at the very time the plants require to have it. Go over the vines in May and deprive them of all the branches that crowd each other; six inches to twelve apart is proper distance to lay in young wood; rub off all others, using only the finger and thumb in the operation; tie in the shoots as they advance, and top them as soon as they have made two eyes' growth beyond the fruit, except the leaders, as above intimated.

There is nothing in the above that is not perfectly simple, and may be put in practice by any farmer, along every fence rail.

FOREIGN GRAPE.

This is the *Vitis vinifera* of botanists, a fruit of the East, where it luxuriates in profusion, being the food and drink of many of the inhabitants of those countries. In these climates it grows without limit, and even under the dry, genial suns of France and the countries bordering on the Mediterranean Sea, it attains great perfection. This climate, however, is inimical to its growth, and after bearing for a few years, it suddenly dies off. Its perfection can only be attained under glass; but with that as a cover, and a knowledge of the cause and effect of the disease to which it is subject, it will amply repay the attention paid to its culture. For such a purpose we introduce the following varieties:

Black Frontignan.—A very rich-flavored Grape, with a peculiar, musky flavor. Bunches rather small, long and compact. Berries medium size; skin thin, covered with a violet bloom. A good bearer; bunches about one pound weight.

Black Hamburg is the best of all Grapes, taking into consideration its combined qualities of productiveness, large size, and fine flavor. Bunches rather tapering, with two or three shoulders, making what is called a well-shouldered bunch. Berries large, sometimes four inches in circumference, rather round, of a jet black color, but vary very much under different treatment; in a warm, moist, or dry atmosphere, ripening from a pale red to its proper color; skin rather thick. Flesh rich, juicy and melting. It is a very large bunch, weighing three pounds.

Black Prince.—If the Black Hamburg has a rival, it is in this Grape. In this vicinity, growers generally prefer it. Bunches tapering and well shouldered. Berries large, of a fine black, not so closely set on the bunch as the Hamburg. Flesh melting, juicy and high flavored. A great bearer and always colors well. A very large bunch will weigh three pounds; wood strong.

Charges Henling.—A black Grape from the south of France introduced by me four years ago. Bunches long and tapering. Berries medium size; color jet black, with a violet bloom. Flesh melting, very juicy, spicy and sprightly; flavor distinct from any other Grape. A great bearer, either in pots or in the ground; bunches from a pound to a pound and a half.

Chasselas Golden, White Chasselas, Royal Muscadine, White Muscadine, Chasselas de Fontainebleau, with many other names, all belong to two varieties of the Grape, very much assimulated, and in which there is great confusion. Bunches long and tapering, with one or two shoulders. Berries medium size; of a white, changing to a bright, transparent, golden color, when fully exposed to the sun. Flesh tender, melting, rich and sugary. A prolific bearer. We have seen a vine in a pot with twenty-nine bunches of fruit on it.

Decan's Superb.—A new Grape, imported by me three years ago, and promises to be the finest white Grape we have in culture for size and bearing, with an excellent flavor. Bunches large, well shouldered Berries perfectly round, three to four inches in circumference; of a greenish-white color. Flesh and flavor very similar to the Hamburg. A strong grower.

Muscat of Alexandria.—Bunches large, as broad as they are long. Berries oval, of a fine yellowish-white color. Flesh firm, with a rich, sweet, musky flavor, peculiar to this variety; few seeds; requires to be fully transparent before being cut; in fact it is not ripe till it begins to shrivel. Many growers cut it before maturity. A large bunch will weigh two pounds. A very strong grower.

Muscat blanc hatif, or *Early White Muscat.*—A very early sort, with well formed bunches. Berries perfectly round, of a yellow-white color. Flesh very rich, juicy, spicy, and high flavored. A great bearer; large bunches will weigh a pound and a half.

Red Frontignan, or *Grizzly Frontignan.*—Bunches long and tapering. Berries perfectly round, of a copper or red color; medium size, and set thickly on the bunch. Flesh rich, spicy, juicy and excellent. The best of Grapes; when once tasted, if perfectly ripe, it will not be forgotten. The fruit should hang on the vine till it begins to shrivel. A large bunch will weigh a pound and a half.

West's, *St. Peters*, or *Black Lombardy.*—Bunches very long (fifteen inches) if well grown. Berries round, of a dull red color, closely set. Flesh juicy and melting. Will hang on the vines till frost; for this it is valuable. Foliage very much lobed, very large branches. Will weigh two and a half to three pounds. A strong grower and great bearer.

White Frontignan.—In character and flavor like the Red Color of a waxy white, with a fine powdery bloom on the fruit.

White Sweet Water.—Very early. Bunches rather small, as is the fruit. Berries round, of a pale-green, transparent color. Flesh thin, sugary, and sweet. A very distinct sort; large bunches will weigh one pound.

Erections.—We here admit that the above described Grapes cannot be grown in the open air with any degree of success. We therefore propose to give a simple detail for a cheap and permanent structure for their protection. There are few gardens of any pretensions that have not glass sash for hot-beds, pits, &c., during Winter. By way of economy, and to suit those who are parsimonious in rural affairs, we propose erecting a building to suit those sashes, which generally remain unemployed during the season from April to November, the very time that the Grape vines require their aid. Admit that the sashes of the frames are six feet long, and those of the pit are seven feet, these, according to Fig. 25, will cover a Grapery nine feet high at the back, ten feet wide, and seven feet high in front, allowing two feet for a low front wall, or plank. This Grapery may be of any length, and can be placed against any wall, building, or good permanent fence, at very little cost; and from it heavy crops of Grapes may be obtained every year. In the Winter season, the vines are to be laid down, after being pruned, in any convenient position, and protected by hay, straw, or boards. In April the vines can be tied up, and the sashes put on them whenever they can be spared from the frames and pits. For the admission of air, a portion of the sash can be moveable and fixed with springs, or hooks and staples.

Fig. 25.

Soil.—There is very little difference of opinion in regard to the nature of the soil genial to the growth and maturity of the Grape. All agree that it should be light and porous, on a dry bottom. The great Grape-growing countries are of that nature, and the vineyards are all planted on rising ground or declivities. The various modes of accomplishing this, is frequently very ludicrous. A great pit is prepared, three to four feet deep, filled with one or two feet of stones, bricks, and other rough material, over which is put a mixture of offal, bones, lime, and other rich manures, with a *small* portion of good, virgin earth. In such receptacles the roots very soon rot, the vines become weak, and finally, after a few years of meagre existence, they die—as might have been expected. If we could make a choice of locality, or even no choice, the most appropriate place on level ground would be, to plant the vines on the surface, or, in other words make the vine border above the ground. It would then always be dry and sweet, and if too dry, water might be given when required. Soils for the growth of this plant must be dry, and free from excess of moisture at any season. The excrementitious matter discharged from the roots of a vine is very great, and if this be given out in cold, retentive soils, they soon become diseased, and a pale and languid vegetation ensues. If, therefore, the bottom is not naturally dry, make it so by draining. Having obtained a dry bottom, by rough materials of any description, cover it to the desired height with fresh turf from a rich pasture, and dig in one-fourth of well-decomposed manure, at least one year old, interspersing it with a few bones of any description, oyster shells, road scrapings from the turnpike, or any other enriching material that undergoes slow decomposition. The whole must be repeatedly turned, and allowed to settle before the vines are planted. Extreme caution has to be used in administering bone dust, slaughter-house offal, and other rich manures, especially if the vines are to be planted in it the same season. The surface of the soil should have a descent to carry off rains and snows. Never crop vine borders, nor tread much upon them. Have a trellis walk laid on the soil, for the daily operations of training, tieing, pruning, &c. Stir up the surface of the border once a year with the fork, and give it a dressing of manure. From these remarks it must not be inferred that vines will not grow unless in richly prepared soils. They will grow well in poor, dry, sandy soils, provided they have annually a good portion of rich vegetable or animal matter dug into them every Autumn, and a covering of manure during Winter—the rains passing through which will strengthen the soil and enable it to give great growths and good crops.

Propagation.—This is frequently done by layers, of which we have given a hint under the culture of Native Grapes; also by cuttings of last year's wood; but the best method of growing fine plants is by the single eye. This is the favorite mode of propagating plants for fruiting. Early in February or March we cut the shoots of the preceding year's wood into eyes, leaving about an inch on each side of the eye, plant these with their eyes uppermost into pots, and place them under glass, either in cold or hot frames prepared for the purpose, or in the window of a warm room, where they will be carefully watered. These eyes may easily be made to grow ten or twelve feet the first season, by constant repotting and watering with liquid manure. Plants grown by this method are decidedly the best rooted, forming more capillary fibres, consequently more nutritious support to the vine is absorbed; they form shorter joints, and are capable of producing a greater quantity of fruit. We have seen a plant of the Black Hamburg, only eighteen months from the eye, have nine bunches, weighing about eight pounds.

Transplanting.—If Grape vines have been cultivated in pots, they may be transplanted at any period of the year, though we give preference to the months of October, November, March or April. Admitting the ground is fully prepared, dig out a place for the reception of the roots, eighteen inches deep, and as wide as the roots require, to lay them, at their full length, without bending or twisting in any manner. If any of them are broken or diseased, cut them off. Keep the roots near the surface, distributing among them fine earth give each three or four gallons of water, allow it to subside when fill up with earth and press it down gently with the foot In such a house as we have figured, one plant to each sash will be enough. The back of the house may be planted with Figs, which should be covered up in Winter, in the same manner as the vines. It is absolutely necessary for the health of the vine that it should be planted where the sun will fully shine upon it during some hours of the day. We have often observed small vines planted in front of the house, where they are entirely shaded from the sun, and had to struggle for weeks or months before they reached the full light and air. In such a case it is preferable to grow the plants in pots, till they are the required height. The first season's growth should be confined to one stem only, carefully cutting off all lateral shoots within two eyes of the main stem.

WINTER PRUNING.—This subject is extensively treated on by all writers on the vine, in the horticulture of Great Britain; and those who have undertaken the subject in this country appear to adopt their words. It may do in some soils and latitudes, but when put in practice here, many of the eyes intended for fruiting the coming season start to growth. The error we will take the liberty to point out. In the preceding paragraph we advise the first season's growth to be confined to one stem; this having been done, cut this shoot down to the bottom of the glass, and allow two shoots to grow from it the next season, and take one bunch of fruit from the strongest shoot, if it shows any. These shoots are to be trained as far as they will grow. Writers say, "top them when one-third, or at farthest, half-way up the rafter:" if this is done in our climate, and the vines in strong health, one-half of the eyes below the stoppings will grow at once, ruining the vine for one year. Our climate elaborates the juices of the plant so fully that a stoppage of its growth has two results, viz.—either destroying the roots or causing a greater reproduction of wood; which in this case is a decided injury. The next Winter cut the weakest shoot to about one eye from the previous year's wood; and the strongest lay in two or three feet of the past season's growth. This portion will have ten or twelve eyes, all of which will break and produce fruit. Take only one bunch from each eye; the other shoot allow to grow its full length without fruit during the season. The next Winter cut back the strong shoot that has produced the large crop to within two eyes of the old wood, and allow one shoot to grow therefrom. The strong shoot is to be laid in, or cut back to two or three feet long for fruiting; one shoot to be trained without fruit for the next year's crop. There may be on the vine four shoots, or the number required, one-half of which lay in to fruit every year, and cut back the other half for fruiting the following season. This is termed the *long cane system*, and is the one we recommend.

Spur System of Pruning, which is exceedingly simple in detail and practice, and the largest crops of Grapes we have ever seen, were from vines trained on this mode. It is as follows: Allow one shoot to extend from the plant, the whole height of the house. If every thing is in good order, this shoot will be at least three inches round. If under, there is a deficiency; cut it back, and give it another year's growth. If over it, the vines are *too* strong, cut this shoot to about four feet of the old wood; from the sides of this stem, young shoots or spurs push forth, which bear fruit. Take only one bunch from each, and stop the growth two eyes above the bunches. At each Winter pruning, these spurs are cut back, leaving two or three eyes to each. These again send out other spurs; take one bunch from each, and so continue from year to year, and you will have fruit in great abundance, though not so fine as on the former method.* Many err in this system in taking two bunches of fruit from each eye, instead of one only. Winter pruning should always be done as soon as the leaves have fallen, otherwise the vine is deprived of matter which would have been

* Since the above was prepared for the press, we have had an interview with one of the best grape-growers under glass, in the country, at whose Grapery, last year, we saw fruit of the finest quality, in regard to color, size, and flavor. He adopts both methods of pruning, but greatly prefers the *cane* training as being most simple—the vine having only one or two wounds made on it, the fruit swelling faster, coloring better, and maturing two weeks before that of the spur pruning, where the comparison was fair; being without fire heat. He also syringes his vines freely, till the fruit is about the size of peas, and never afterwards. He never saw red-spider on his vines, and very rarely mildew. Observe that all our remarks apply to grape houses without artificial heat.

stored up in the remaining parts. Never prune back wood of the present year to one eye, as is usually recommended, but leave a long spur of three eyes; the eye or bud nearest the old stem is frequently blind, and even if it does show fruit, it is not so fine as the eyes farther up the shoot; but be careful to retain the best, and rub off the remainder at the earliest stage of growth, always encouraging the base bud shoot to be retained for the next season's operation. *Summer pruning* must be strictly attended to, stopping every shoot two leaves above the bunch, after which laterals, or new shoots, will soon be produced. These, stop again every two weeks, to concentrate the energy of the plant on the swelling of the fruit.

THINNING THE FRUIT.—This portion of culture is too frequently neglected. As soon as the berries are the size of small peas, cut out about one-third of them with a pair of sharp-pointed scissors. This will allow the others to swell more freely. Again, before they begin to color, if they appear crowded, thin out the smallest. This will not reduce the weight of the bunch, unless the thinning is carried to extreme. Never touch the fruit after it begins to color. Handling destroys the fine bloom on the fruit, which is a point of beauty. Tieing up the shoulders does not improve the fruit nor add to the effect.

ROUTINE OF CULTURE under glass, without fire heat. As soon as the frosty nights are over, clean all the wood-work by washing, or white-washing. Lift up the vines from where they have been laid all Winter, and wash them with strong soap-suds, or soft soap and tobacco water, rubbing off all the loose bark, and cleaning them thoroughly. After which tie them up to the places appropriate for them. Every morning after they begin to grow, give them a syringing with water, about an hour after sun-rise, provided the sashes are on the house. If the sashes are not on, they do not require it so frequently. About the end of April, or first of May, the sashes must necessarily be put on to protect the blossom, encourage the growth, and prevent injury in cold nights.

When the fruit has set, the vines may be syringed every afternoon, about four o'clock, having previously shut up the house, not to be opened again till the sun has fairly tempered the atmosphere next day, which will generally be from nine to ten o'clock, if the house fronts south, when air must be given by the top sashes, not allowing the thermometer to go higher than from 90 to 110 degrees.

During the warm, cloudy days of July and August, mildew is sure to appear, and has frequently accomplished great destruction before it is discovered. It is readily known by a yellow, sickly transparency on the leaf, or a greasy, soft feel when you lay hold of it. The best cure is to give copious syringings of water, twice a day, giving plenty of air, to the house from ten to three o'clock, in sunshine. If it has far gone, pour four gallons of boiling water over five pounds of flower of sulphur, stir it well, and after allowing it to settle, mix a fourth of this water with that which is used for syringing, which will entirely kill all mildew. Never leave the doors open for any length of time; it causes cold draughts of air through the vines. Cease syringing as soon as the fruit begins to color. Give water to the roots every week, whilst they are in a growing state, till the fruit has fully swelled.

The hints we have thrown out on the culture of this truly luscious fruit will, we think, enable any one to grow it at least to a small degree of perfection; and with a mediocrity of caution and observation, good and regular crops may be obtained for either pleasure or profit.

NECTARINE.

Amygdalis, var.—*Brugnon*, Fr.—*Nectarpfirsche*, Ger.

I have never considered this fruit as any other production than a garden variety of the Peach, from which it is only distinguished by the smoothness of the skin. Many highly wrought descriptions of it have extolled it as being finer flavored than the Peach. If so, it has not been our good fortune to have tasted such: on the contrary, we consider it an inferior variety of that fruit, and of an inferior flavor. Neither will the Nectarine ever be so universally cultivated, being generally of a smaller size; and the smoothness of its skin is favorable to the attacks of the Curculio, which destroys them in quantities every season, stinging the fruit even worse than the Plum; and until we can entirely extirpate these animals, it will be a scarce fruit in this vicinity. The following five sorts, from about twenty, will form a select collection.

Boston.—An American variety, by Mr. Lewis, of Boston, and brought into notice by S. G. Perkins, Esq. Color bright yellow, with red cheek. A sweet and pleasant flavor, large size. Freestone.

Downton.—Fruit of a greenish-white color, with a dark red cheek. Flesh very rich, melting, and juicy; large size, and the very best quality. Freestone.

New White.—Is of a creamy-white color, medium size. Flesh white, rich, melting, and rather juicy. A freestone.

Pitmaston Orange.—Fruit medium size, of a bright golden-yellow color, with a red cheek. Flesh deep yellow, melting, rich and sweet, fine flavor. Freestone.

Red Roman.—One of the oldest and most celebrated varieties. Fruit large, of a yellowish-green color, with a dull red cheek, specked with brown. Flesh firm, pale yellow, juicy, rich and very high flavored. Equal to the Downton, but is a clingstone.

Violette hative.—Fruit very similar to the former, with a greenish-white flesh. A freestone.

They all ripen from the 1st of August to the 1st of Sept.

Cultivation.—The soil and culture suitable for the Peach perfectly agrees with the Nectarine. It is also budded in the same manner, and if practicable should always be obtained on the Plum stock

PEACH.

Amy'gdalis Pérsica.—Pecher, Fr.—*Pfirschbaum*, Ger.

It is to be supposed that every inhabitant of the United States is familiar with the Peach. In both flavor and appearance it is legitimately a fruit of this country, though a foreigner—a native of Persia, where it has been known from the earliest ages. History says it was first sent by the king of Persia into Egypt, with the view of poisoning the inhabitants, with whom he was then at war: and, strange to say, most of the ancient writers describe this fruit as possessing deleterious qualities. The leaves of the tree, however, contain prussic acid. From the days of Virgil the fruit has been considered of first-rate excellence, which few will dispute; and the Peaches of this country are equal to any in the world. With the purposes for which they are used every one is familiar. They are cultivated in the States of New Jersey and Delaware by the tens of thousands of acres—one family alone employing a steamboat in the Peach season, to carry their fruit to market. There are hundreds of varieties cultivated—many orchards of natural fruit without names, and other orchards of a more profitable character, containing only a very few select sorts, known for their superior merits. The following twenty kinds we note as being such, whilst we will not deny that there may be others equally as good in other parts of the country, unknown to us.

Alberge, or *Yellow Rare-ripe.*—Color bright yellow, red cheek, round form, large size. Ripe early in August—*free.*

Columbia.—Color brownish-yellow, striped red, round form, large size. Ripe about the middle of September—*free.*

Early Melocoton (Crawford's).—Color brownish-yellow; red cheek; oval form. Ripe 15th August—*free.*

Early York.—Color dark red; round form; medium size; excellent quality; a great bearer. Ripe 0th of August—*free.*

Foxe's Seedling.—Color greenish-white; red cheek; round form; large size. Ripe early in September.

Favorite (Reeve's).—Color yellowish-red; round form. Ripe early in September—*free.*

George 4th.—Color greenish-white; red cheek; round form; large size. Ripe end of August—*free.*

Grosse Mignonne, or *Royal George*—with about twenty other names, is a large round Peach, rather flattened; color greenish-yellow; a mottled red cheek; flesh white, red at the stone. The first Peach we became familiar with, and have seen it eleven and a half inches in circumference. Ripe in August—*free.*

Imperial (Darby).—Color yellow-brown, with dull red cheek; round form. Ripe middle of September—*free.*

Late Heath.—Color white; faint red cheek; oval form. Ripe in October—*cling.*

Late Melocoton (Crawford's).—Color dull yellow; dark red cheek; roundish form. Ripe 12th to 25th September—*free.*

La Grange.—Color greenish-white; oval form. Ripe 10th September—*free.*

Morris White.—Color pure white; oval form. Ripe early in September—*free.*

Nonpareil (Scott's).—Dull yellow; red cheek; roundish form. Ripe 15th September—*free.*

Old Mixon (*free*).—Color dull red; oval form. Ripe early in September.

Old Mixon (*cling*).—Color dull red; round form. Ripe early in September.

Red Cheek Melocoton—Color yellowish-green; dull red cheek; oval form. Ripe 18th September—*free.*

Red Rare-Ripe.—Color greenish-white; dark red cheek; oval form. Ripe end of August—*free.*

Rodman's Red.—Color dull red; oval form. Ripe end of September and 1st of October—*cling.*

Tippecanoe.—Color bright yellow, with red cheek; oval form. Ripe 10th to 20th September—*cling*.

PROPAGATION.—This is of the simplest character. It is usually performed by planting the stones (or pits), in November, about two inches deep, in rich, light, or sandy soil. These nearly all vegetate in the Spring, and can be budded the following September, or about the end of August. They are then headed down close to the bud, early in the Spring, when they will make a growth of from three to nine feet the first season, with lateral branches all up the stem. In some parts of Ohio, Kentucky, and Mississippi, the stones are planted in November, budded the end of the following June, headed down in July, and make a growth of four to six feet all within one year of the stone being planted. These operations are all performed on the Peach-stone. The tree is consequently short-lived; but being so readily replaced, that is not generally considered of much consequence. However, we would prefer budding for our own use on the Plum stock. The tree will live half a century thereon, and will not be subject to the Borer, which is a great enemy to the Peach stock.

PLANTING.—If we wish to reap the fruit, we must prepare the soil. As the foundation is laid, so will the erection stand. Plough or dig your soil deep; manure well the year previous; plant your trees twenty feet apart, which will take one hundred to the acre. Our remarks on planting Apples will apply here. Cultivate the ground with a light crop, giving manure every two years.

PRUNING.—This is very indifferently attended to in the Peach. The trees are allowed to grow at random—long, straggling branches, with the fruit at the extremity, bending them to the ground, and never thinned out. The result is, the first storm breaks half of the limbs, and the fruit does not grow over half its size, ripening prematurely, and commanding about one-third the price of full-grown, well-ripened fruit. It is twenty years since we pruned Peach trees, in the same manner as we have described for Currant bushes, keeping the young wood thin, and shortening every growth in the Fall or Winter pruning. The trees are thereby made more compact, not so liable to be broken, and produce finer fruit; the beauty of the tree is improved, and its age lengthened.

The Borer, or *Peach-worm*, is very destructive to this tree. The insect, according to Say, is a dark-blue, four-winged, slender moth, depositing its egg during the Summer months around the tree, close to the surface of the ground. Ashes have been long used as a protective against this destroyer, with very good effect; and recently half a peck of air-slacked lime, heaped round the tree during the month of May, is considered as a perfect antidote, effectually securing the tree against its enemy. The lime is spread over the ground after the fall of the leaf, and a fresh supply given every year at the above period.

There is a disease called "*The Yellows*," very prevalent in some orchards, which is attributed to a variety of causes. The main one, we presume, will generally be found in ungenial soil, and overcropping of the trees. We say, thin out the crop—do not allow one fruit to be within two inches of its neighbor. Shorten the young growths of the tree by Winter pruning, and cut out others where they are too thick, thereby giving plenty of air to all parts of the tree. Manure every other year and crop light. With such a routine of culture the Yellows will be a stranger. Trees that produce a crop of fruit which is yearly carried off the ground, must have some return, by enriching the soil, either by manure from the stable-yard, or rich composts of lime, marl, plaster, &c.

PEAR.

Pyrus commūnis.—Poirier, Fr.—*Birnbaum*, Ger.

The present period is a very exciting one on the culture of this fruit, which ranks in flavor next to the Peach; but in point of healthfulness and general utility, for domestic purposes, it will be second to the Apple. In its wild state it is equally disseminated with that fruit, but we doubt of its culture ever being so universal, it being more subject to diseases, especially to blight. Some soils are entirely noxious to it, while others nourish it to extreme old age. It is also longer in coming to a fruit-bearing state than the Apple, though some of the recent kinds appear to produce fruit as early as the third or fourth years from the bud, and frequently the second year from the graft. As a dessert, or table fruit, it is preferable to the Apple, and is also very important for cooking purposes. In some countries *Perry* is made from the fruit, in the same manner that we do cider, for which purpose there are special productive varieties. Within the past twenty years the immense multiplication of sorts renders it a very intricate task to select, from the multitude, a few well adapted for general cultivation, because the variety that does best in some sections of the country nearly fails in others, and those that are described from the fruit, as being the best in size and flavor, on trial prove to be the worst in productiveness. One of the most celebrated horticulturists of the age, who does all his "own thinking," writing to me from "Boston, September 20, 1846," says: "There is, in my view, too much of a rage for new fruits, and the old superior varieties are neglected. Of Pears they have here near two hundred varieties, and possibly twenty of fair quality." I will however give an outline description of a few, slightly transcending that limited number, and vouch for all of them being of the very best.

Summer Pears. *Madeline.*—Fruit pear-shaped, rather under the medium size, with a long foot-stalk. Color pale yellow-green. Flesh white, very rich, juicy, and high flavored; a great bearer. Ripe 20th July.

Bloodgood.—Fruit rounding, flat at the eye, medium size; color yellow, with a brown cheek. Flesh yellowish-white, rich and sugary, with a fine, aromatic flavor. Ripe 1st of August.

Julienne.—Fruit rather under medium size; oval form; color bright yellow. Flesh buttery and juicy. Ripe early in August. Fruit should be plucked a few days before ripe.

Tyson.—Fruit medium size; pyramidal form; color dull greenish-yellow. Flesh white, sweet, melting, and very juicy, with a most delightful flavor. Ripe from the 15th to the 25th of August. A figure of this variety is given in Hovey's Magazine for November, 1846, but much too small for the general size of the fruit. The original tree, now over fifty years of age, stands in Jenkintown, Pa., and measures six feet in circumference, at three feet from the ground, and is a noble specimen of strong, upright growth. The fruit has been sold in Philadelphia Market for nearly twenty years, but till recently very little notice has been taken of it. We would like to taste a finer, early pear than this.

Moyamensing.—Fruit full, medium size, of a roundish-oval form; lemon color, with occasional blotches and lines of russet Flesh buttery, melting, and well flavored. In eating from the middle of July till the end f August. Originated in the garden of J. B. Smith, Esq., of this place.

Washington.—Another American Pear, of first rate quality. *Fruit* medium size; oval form; of a pale straw color, covered with brown dots. Flesh firm, white, melting and juicy. Ripe end of August and 1st of September. Downing's figure of this fruit and description is perfectly accurate, though there is plenty of evidence to show that this tree must have been known forty years ago. I have seen grafted trees about fifty feet high, and a stem four feet in circumference.

Bartlett.—Fruit very large, regular pyramidal form; color pale lemon-yellow, with a faint blush next the sun. Flesh white, very juicy, buttery, and high flavored. Ripe first of September.

Autumn Pears.—*Seckel.*—Fruit under medium size; color of a brownish-yellow, with a russety blush next the sun. Flesh yellowish-white, juicy, rich, and peculiarly high flavored. In rich, loamy soil the fruit is medium-sized. The parent tree still lives about three miles from Philadelphia. Ripe about first of September.

Butter or *White Doyenne,* with about twenty-five other names. Fruit over medium size; very regularly formed, round-oval; color greenish-yellow, with a blush cheek. Flesh white, fine, buttery flavor, juicy and rich. Ripe 10th to the 25th of September, varies very much in different soils.

Beurre de Capiumont.—Fruit under medium size, regularly formed; color pale yellow, with a dull red cheek. Flesh buttery, sweet, melting, and high flavored. Ripe in September or early in October.

Beurre Bosc. —Fruit large, regularly pyramidal; color brownish-yellow, with a reddish-brown cheek. Flesh white, melting, rich, and highly perfumed flavor. Ripe from September to the end of October. *A noble fruit.*

Fondante d'Automne.—Fruit medium size, half oval; color yellowish-green, slightly russeted. Flesh very juicy, rich and delicious. Ripe in September. We have not seen this fruit, but give it a place from the high character given to it by M. P. Wilder, Esq., President of the Massachusetts Horticultural Society, who is one of the best judges.

Beurre Diel.—Fruit large, of an oval form; color pale yellow, when fully ripe, dotted with brown. Flesh yellowish-white, rich, sugary, and high flavored. Ripe from September to the end of November.

Marie Louise.—Fruit fully medium size; color greenish-yellow, with russety cheek. Flesh white, very buttery, rich, and high flavored. Ripe from September to October. We have had large crops of this fruit on trees only eight feet high.

Duchesse d'Angouleme.—Fruit very large; long oval, with an uneven surface; color dull greenish-yellow. Flesh white, buttery, very rich, and high flavored. Ripe in October and November, and is frequently over one pound weight.

Dix.—An American fruit, of large pyramidal form; color dull yellow, dotted with russet. Flesh rich, juicy, sugary, and melting. Ripe in October.

Urbaniste.—Fruit medium size; pyramidal form; color grayish-yellow. Flesh yellowish-white, rich, melting, very juicy, and high flavored. Ripe in October and November.

WINTER PEARS. *Columbia.*—An American fruit, very large, oval form; color pale greenish-yellow. Flesh white, melting, juicy and sweet, aromatic flavor. Ripe November to December.

Beurre d'Aremberg.—Fruit above medium size; oval form, with an uneven surface. Flesh white, rich, melting, and luscious flavor. Ripe in November and December.

Chaumontel.—Fruit large; oval form, with an irregular surface; color yellowish-green, with a brownish-red cheek. Flesh melting, buttery, sweet, and luscious flavor. Ripe November to January.

Glout Morceau.—Fruit large; regular, of a long, oval form; color pale greenish-yellow. Flesh white, smooth, rich, and sugary. Ripe December to January.

Lawrence.—This peculiar variety originated on Long Island. Fruit above medium size, rather oval; color pale yellowish-green, spotted with brown. Flesh yellowish-white, melting, juicy, very rich, and sugary flavor. (*Downing on Fruits.*) We have not seen this fruit, but have been informed by the Messrs. Parsons, of Flushing, that some of the fruit begins to ripen in November, while others continue ripening till March.

Passe Colmar, with about twenty other names. Fruit large,

of regular pear-shape; color yellowish-green, with a brownish-russet. Flesh creamy-white, with a buttery, rich, juicy, aromatic flavor. Ripe in December.

Winter Nelis.—Fruit medium size, roundish form; color greenish-yellow, with a russety cheek. Flesh yellowish-white, smooth, buttery, abounding in a rich, aromatic juice. Ripe in December and January.

Beurre Easter.—Fruit large, oval form; color yellowish-brownish-green, with a russety cheek. Flesh white, smooth, buttery, juicy, and very sweet. Ripe in January, February, and March.

Beurre de Ranz.—Fruit above medium size, of a long, pyramidal shape. Color rough, dark green, (rather untempting.) Flesh greenish-white, melting, rich, and juicy. Ripe in March, April, and May.

Propagation and Culture.—The Pear, like the Apple, is propagated by seeds, budding, or grafting. By the former process, many new sorts have made their appearance in this country and Europe, of very superior quality, within the past twenty years. Those of the United States are not surpassed in their season by any others, and should always have the preference when plantations are made; their constitution and productiveness being acclimated, there is not likely any disappointment to arise from barrenness or other defects. There has, within these few years past, arisen up among us, some genuine pomological spirits, that will bring into notice many native sorts of this fruit that are at present either obscure, or entirely unknown. It can be grafted or budded with great success on its own stock, and also on the Quince, and with partial success on the Apple. Grafting early in Spring, and budding in July and August. Every Pear tree of an inferior description should be headed down, or cut back in the branches, to within a few feet of the stem, and grafted with finer and more productive sorts The new kinds will produce fruit at once. The result would be, instead of Pears being worth twenty-five cents per bushel, they would at least be worth twelve times that amount.

Planting the Pear, is precisely as described for the Apple; though they will admit of being as close as twenty-five or thirty feet. The finest trees we know, grow on a light. loamy soil, three feet deep, with a sandy, gravelly bottom. The worst soil we have observed them on, is composed of a sandy, thin, light nature, with a cold or wet bottom.

Pruning.—This tree, in the first few years of its growth, after being transplanted, requires the aid of the knife in directing the formation of its head; but when once formed, it requires no further care, unless to keep the interior of the head thinned out, to allow a free circulation of air. Avoid making large amputations when pruning. The saw and the axe are dangerous implements in the hands of unskilful orchardists.

Blight is the only disease in this country that attacks the Pear. Its remedies are not yet fully tested, and at present are very conflicting and unsatisfactory. The fact, that in some situations they are more subject to it than in others, shows conclusively, I think, that it is a local and not an atmospheric disease.

The *Insect Blight* appears in July and August, and frequently has done much mischief before being detected—whole limbs dying, as it were, instantly. *Remedy*, examine your trees frequently in those months, and as soon as you detect any of the limbs with the leaves having a drooping appearance, and in habit altogether different from the other portions of the tree, cut it off close to the main limb, and have it destroyed. The insect has girdled the pith, and prevented the circulation of the sap.

Gathering the Fruit. Rather more attention ought to be given to the collecting and keeping the fruit of the Pear tree than it generally receives. All Summer fruit should be pulled a few days before maturity, and put carefully away, either in a fruit room or closet, till it ripens. Autumn fruits should be gathered eight days before being ripe, and put away in cotton, paper, or other dry material, in the dark. They will thereby greatly improve in color and flavor, and will be in use longer. Winter fruit should hang on the tree till frost, then be carefully pulled, and put away for two weeks; when they should be wiped with a cloth, rolled up in cotton or paper, packed in boxes, or barrels of dry sand, and stored in a dry cellar or room, where they will not be severely frozen. Their flavor and color is greatly improved by this method. In the Winter season, fruit should be brought into a warm apartment a few days before using, keeping it invariably in the dark.

PLUM.

Prunùs doméstica.—*Prune,* Fr.—*Pflaumenbaum,* Ger.

There are some species of the Plum found in Asia, Europe, and America. It is an ancient fruit, held in high estimation by the Romans, who amused themselves (as history says) by grafting the Plum on the Apple. We are not surprised at these and other notions, for it is current in the present age that black Roses can be obtained by budding on Black Currant bushes. When they grow, no doubt they will be black. It is not acknowledged to be a first class, healthy fruit, though it is admitted "they will not injure strong constitutions." When perfectly ripe, a few can be eaten to advantage, as they tend to keep the system open. The bark of the Wild Plum is used as a substitute for Peruvian Bark, in cases of intermitting fever. The fruit is considered indispensable as a conserve. Nothing of the kind can equal Green Gage jelly, and preserved Washington Plums. The following are indispensable for a good collection:

Bleecker's Gage.—Raised in the State of New York. *Fruit* oval, of medium size; color yellow, with white specks. Flesh yellow, rich, sweet and luscious. Ripe, end of August. Free.—*Downing.*

Coe's Golden Drop.—An English variety. *Fruit* very large; long-oval; color rich, golden-yellow, with numerous brown dots. Flesh yellow, very rich and luscious. Ripe about the 10th of September, and will keep till October. A cling; will not do for preserving.

Columbia.—A New York seedling. *Fruit* very large; round, fine form; color brownish-purple, with numerous specks. Flesh orange, if perfectly ripe, rich and sugary. Free. Ripe about the end of August.—*Downing.*

Imperial Gage, or *Flushing Gage.*—Raised at Prince's nursery, Flushing. *Fruit* oval; medium size; color green, tinged with yellow next the sun. Flesh yellowish-green, rich, juicy, and delicious. Free. Ripe about the 24th of July.

Green Gage, or *Reine Claude.*—The Plum of Plums. *Fruit* rather under size; color greenish-yellow. Flesh green, very rich, juicy, melting, and very luscious. A great bearer. Free stone. Ripe about the 10th of August.

Huling's Superb.—A native of this country. *Fruit* very large; round-oval; color greenish-yellow. Flesh same color, firm, rich, and well flavored. A great bearer. Free stone. An excellent table or kitchen fruit. Ripe 4th of August.

Morocco.—*Fruit* round; medium size; color dark violet-purple. Flesh yellow, juicy, sharp, and well flavored. Ripe about the 24th of July.

Nectarine, or *Caledonian.*—*Fruit* very large; oval; color purple, with a fine bloom. Flesh yellow, rich, and sharp flavor. Ripe about the 8th of August.

Orleans Early.—*Fruit* round; medium size. Flesh greenish-yellow; color marbled-red, with a purple cheek; sharp, rich flavor. A free stone. A great bearer. Ripe about the first of August.

Jefferson.—An Albany seedling, and, according to report (we have not seen it), one of the finest sorts. *Fruit* large, fine, oval form; color golden-yellow, with a red cheek. Flesh deep orange, very rich, juicy, and high flavored; parts freely from the stone. Ripe about the 25th of August.

Purple Gage.—*Fruit* round, medium size; color reddish-crimson, dotted. Flesh pale orange, rich, juicy, and high flavored. A free stone. Ripe about the 15th of September.

Quetsche, or *German Prune.*—*Fruit* very large, regularly oval; color dark blue-violet when fully ripe. The skin separates very readily from the flesh, and makes a first rate dessert or kitchen fruit. Ripe about the 10th of September.

Imperatrice.—*Fruit* oval, above medium size; color deep purple, covered with bloom. Flesh firm, rich, and sugary, adhering to the stone. Ripe about the first of October.

Washington (*Bolmar's*).—A New York seedling. *Fruit* very large; round-oval; color dull greenish-yellow. Flesh yellow, firm, sweet, and luscious, separating readily from the stone. Ripe about the 15th of August.

Wine Sour.—*Fruit* medium size, roundish-oval; color purple. Flesh bright red, exceedingly juicy. A great bearer, and the best Plum for cooking. Ripe in September.

It must be conceded that the character of the Plum is, in some measure, choice, good, or indifferent, according to situation, climate, and soil; yet we contend that bad soil and situation will not entirely obliterate the good qualities of a choice fruit.

Culture.—The best soil for the Plum is a strong, loamy soil, on a dry bottom. In such they grow well and produce fine crops.

Plant them at twenty-five feet apart, if in the orchard; but if for family use, they should be planted on some paved yard, or other situation, where the fallen fruit will be carefully destroyed.

If the general nature of the soil is sandy, it will be benefited by a compost of very old manure and meadow earth, in equal proportions, being incorporated with it, where the trees are to be planted.

PROPAGATION is done with the greatest facility by planting the stones in the month of October, about an inch deep. These vegetate the following season, and can be transplanted into a convenient part of the garden in rows, to be budded the second year, in the month of July, in a period of cloudy, moist weather. They can also be grafted very early in Spring, by either whip or wedge grafting, as recommended for the Apple; but it must be observed, that stone-fruit does not take so readily by grafting as budding. Useless varieties of the Plum should be cut back, as advised for the Pear; they will then make vigorous shoots, a portion of which can be saved and budded with choice varieties. Where there is not much room, and a variety of fruit wanted, we strongly advise several sorts of fruit to be worked on one tree; by adopting this practice with all kinds of fruit trees, a great variety can be obtained in a very small space. In favorable soils their growth is rapid. There is, within fifty feet of where I write, a tree thirteen years from the stone, that is budded with four sorts, produces a large crop every season, is now thirty feet high, and two feet from the ground the stem measures three feet in circumference.

PRUNING is performed as directed for Pears; but large amputations should only be made in July, August, or September. At that period the wounds will readily heal over.

INSECTS.—The great and only foe of this tree is the Curculio, or Plum-Weevil. A preventive to its ravages has not been discovered. We observe trees planted in pavements, or near to dwellings, are not so subject to its attack as those in cultivated ground or gardens. Some kinds are also more subject to it than others. With us, the following are entirely destroyed by it: Coes' Golden Drop, Magnum Bonum, Kirk's Late Red, and Bingham; while the Green Gage, Morocco, Wine Sour, Orleans, and Washington, are not or but slightly, injured. As a cure, fifteen or twenty pounds of salt, or salt brine, is strongly recommended by some. It is laid under the tree early in Autumn. This is to destroy the insects, which lie under the surface of the ground all Winter. We doubt not but repeated doses of this will destroy them.

QUINCE.

Py̆rus Cydōnia.—*Coignassier*, Fr.—*Quittenbaum*, Ger.

THE Quince is supposed to be the Golden Apples of the ancients. It is a native of Austria, and is believed to have been cultivated in Britain three hundred years. Pliny writes, in his time, of their growing wild in hedge-rows, so large as to weigh down the boughs to the ground. Moderns use it only after being stewed, baked, or preserved. Quince marmalade is a favorite conserve, and Quince wine has been known to cure obstinate asthmatic complaints. There are only two varieties and a species that are worth notice.

Apple, or *Orange Quince.*—The fruit large, of a round-oval shape; skin very smooth; color, when ripe, a bright golden-yellow. A clean growing tree and a great bearer. Ripe in September and October.

Portugal Quince.—*Fruit* round, large size; color bright yellow. A strong-growing tree and bears a fair crop. This variety is used as stocks on which to bud or graft Pears; they fruit earlier upon it, and are much dwarfed by the process. It is a very general practice with the French, and for small gardens may be done to advantage in this country, but will not do for orchards.

Pyrus Sinensis, or *Chinese Quince.*—Shrub of upright growth, with pink flowers. *Fruit* very large, long-oval, smooth and regularly formed color greenish-yellow. Flesh firm, rather dry. Ripe about the end of October. A beautiful preserve, of a bright pink color, can be made from the fruit. A specimen before me is really beautiful.

PROPAGATION.—This is readily accomplished by layers or cuttings, as they root in either way very freely. Lay down the shoots early in Spring, or during the mild Winter months, and they will be rooted by the following November, when they can be planted out into rows till they are strong enough to be removed to the orchard. *Cuttings* taken off the old plants of the past year's wood, or even wood of two years old, cut into lengths of about eight inches and planted into moist ground, will root the first year and soon attain to be good plants.

SOIL.—A heavy, loamy soil, is said to be the best for the Quince. This is not borne out by results. The finest fruit I have ever seen is grown on deep, sandy loam, manured every season. If they are not well cultivated, they get knotty and deformed, producing fruit of like character.

PRUNING.—Very little assistance is required from the knife, unless to give a direction to the formation of the tree, and for shortening any shoots that extend beyond the regular bounds.

RASPBERRY.

Rubus idèus.—Framboisier, Fr.—*Himbeerestrauch*, Ger.

SOME species of this plant are natives of all temperate countries, and have been much improved by cultivation. Its fruit is extensively used for making syrups, wines, jams, and jellies; it also forms an excellent dessert fruit, considered healthful, refreshing, and cooling. Of late, much has been said and written on the Raspberry; but as yet, we may say, there are but two or three sorts worth general culture.

Red Antwerp.—Canes dark brown, long, short-jointed. *Fruit* fairly thimble-shaped. Flesh firm, rich, juicy, with a fine, sweet flavor. Ripe about the fourth of July. There is a variety called Red Antwerp generally cultivated, with small fruit, readily broken into pieces, and wood of a reddish-brown color.

Franconia is a hardier variety than the former, and does better in colder latitudes. *Fruit* large, conical, of a bright red color. Flesh firm; flavor sharp; rich and abundant. Ripe about the middle of July.

White, or Yellow Antwerp.—*Fruit* nearly as large as the Red Antwerp; of the same shape. Flesh yellow, very tender, rich, and very sweet. Wood yellow; a great bearer.

Fastolff.—Within the past few years this variety though) an old one with a new name) has created quite an excitement in England, and not a little in this country. We fruited it two years ago, and consider it one of the best reds, though we do not think it the very best. *Fruit* very large; of an oval, conical form. Flesh very rich, juice abundant, and makes a beautiful dessert fruit. It will never be a popular market fruit, being so soft that it will not bear carriage, but will hold its place for home consumption. Ripe 4th of July.

Ohio Ever-bearing.—*Fruit* conical; color black; large size, produced in clusters on the points of the shoots. Flesh dark-red, juice not very abundant, produces through the whole season till frost, and quite indispensaable on this account. Wood strong, of a dark purple color.

There are several very astonishing and superior Raspberries raised from seed by an amateur gentleman of this city, some of them of a beautiful orange, and others of a bright amber color, whose true characters will be known in another year.

PROPAGATION.—This is of the easiest character. Give the plants rich, deep, sandy loamy soil, and they will send up an abundance of suckers every season, each of which will form a plant and produce fruit the year following.

PLANTING.—They should be put out in rows three feet apart and four feet from row to row. Two hundred plants is not too many for a family. Give them plenty of manure every year. Dig deep, but not close to the bottom of the plant. A situation partially shaded, or naturally moist, though not wet, is the best locality. A plantation will last twenty years if properly attended to by enriching every year.

PRUNING.—The first fruit I ever pruned was the Raspberry, and it is the only one that can be reduced to a simple rule. In the Autumn cut out all the old wood that produced fruit the past summer, close to the ground; tie up the new shoots to a stake or trellis, about five feet high; then cut off about a foot of the tops of the shoots, and the work is done. In cold situations the plants, after having been deprived of their old wood, have to be laid down all Winter, and covered with earth, Spruce, or Pine branches, till Spring, when they are lifted and tied up as above. The *Ohio* and *Franconia* varieties do not require this protection.

STRAWBERRY.

Fragaria, var.—*Fraisier*, Fr.—*Erdbeerpflanze*, Ger.

THE Strawberry, so called from the ancient practice,—and still continued—of laying straw between the rows to keep the fruit clean. It is not properly a berry, but considered "a fleshy receptacle, studded with seeds." It is a wholesome and most luscious fruit, and wisely distributed by a bountiful hand over nearly every part of the world. Its cultivation has been little regarded till within the past thirty years; and even at the present period is very imperfectly understood. Its healthful influence upon nearly all constitutions, when taken in moderate quantities, is admitted by medical men. The demand for it in a commercial point of view is rapidly on the increase, which has created a desire to know its character and improve its culture. Its uses are generally known. A certain species of beauty is compared to "Strawberries smothered in cream," a portion of the dessert palatable to all, though the beneficial effects of the fruit is most certain when fresh from the vine, unmixed and unadulterated. The immense number of varieties now cultivated renders it rather difficult to select from them a few sorts that will continue the season to the longest possible period. In attempting to do so, however, we give preference to varieties obtained from seed in this country, which resist the vicissitudes of our climate, and give more general satisfaction than any imported variety. Our selection comprises two seedlings of Pennsylvania origin, one of New York, and one of Massachusetts.

Early May—is a pistillate (*female?*) variety. *Fruit* above medium size; color bright red; shape conical; flavor very rich, with a delightful aroma. Ripened last year on the 14th of May (season two weeks later than usual). This variety requires to have a row of the Hudson strawberry planted with it to produce the very great crops of which it is capable. It will be a general market fruit.

Hovey's Seedling.—This pistillate (*female?*) variety is now universally cultivated in every part of the United States, and greatly admired. *Fruit* very large, heart-shaped; color dark red, when fully ripe; flavor good, with a fine aroma. Ripened last year about the 22d of May. This variety requires a few of the Hudson, or some other staminate sort to be planted near it, when it produces extraordinary crops. Is a general market fruit.

Prize Seedling.—One of the finest flavored strawberries in cultivation. A staminate variety, and produces a crop of fruit, when planted alone, of very large size, of a rounded, heart-shaped form. Color dark crimson, when fully ripe, with a polished surface; seeds prominent. Ripened last year on the 20th of May, and continues fully three weeks in bearing; an unusual length of time with us.

Ross' Phœnix.—A staminate plant, producing a crop when planted by itself. *Fruit* very large, and frequently of a cox-comb-shape; of a dark red color, with a smooth, polished surface. Flesh firm, and of a very rich flavor, with a delightful aroma. Ripened last year about the 26th of May.

Monthly Copii.—This variety of the Alpine Strawberry is an improvement on the old sort. The fruit is larger, of a finer flavor, and produces copiously the whole year, and is veritably a monthly Strawberry.

There are several varieties recently produced from seeds in this vicinity, and other parts of the country, which will entirely supplant every foreign sort; and we doubt not may even displace some of those we have named, though they are not yet fully proven.

Propagation of Strawberries from Seed.—Every person who has any partiality for this fruit, that can devote a few hours to their culture in their season, should sow the seeds of the very best kinds any time from August to April, in pots of light earth; water them regularly, and they will be above ground in four or five weeks. After they have attained a few leaves to each, plant them into a piece of rich ground in the garden, about twenty inches apart. The second season they will produce fruit to prove their merits. The seed is obtained by drying the ripe fruit and washing the flesh from the seeds, which are all on the outside of the berry; these seeds, when perfectly dry, will keep three years. *Flowers* that have an entirely green centre are called female, or pistilate—those that have a great many yellow stamens are called male, *or barren plants*—those that have only a portion of stamens around the base of the green, conical centre of the flower, are called staminate or perfect blossoms.

Soil.—All admit that the best soil for this fruit is a deep, light, rich loam, if not naturally deep to be made so by trenching. Rich it must be, if large and good fruit is required.

therefore, prepare the ground the season before, planting and incorporating it with an abundance of manure, to the depth of eighteen inches. The exposure must be entirely free from the shade of trees or buildings. For early crops, plant on an aspect that has an inclination to the south or south-east. For late crops choose the north or west. By this method the Strawberry season is greatly prolonged.

PLANTING.—The periods for performing this is in March and April, or August and September: in either of these months we have been equally successful. Beds four feet wide, each containing three rows, and the plants fifteen inches apart in the row, leaving alleys two and a half feet wide between the beds, for the operations of gathering, weeding, hoeing, &c. Never take any other crop from among them, except a few Radishes or Lettuce, the first season. Destroy the runners after the middle of July, unless they are wanted for plants; hoe them freely, and keep the ground in an open condition. Some light, rough litter should be sprinkled over the plants during Winter, in cold localities. In light soils dig in between the rows every Autumn, a few inches of well-rotted dung; but in strong and deep alluvial soils it may be dispensed with. In dry seasons give the plants a few waterings, after they have done blooming, with any liquid manure, or other rich water, which will greatly promote the swelling of the fruit. A plantation will last three or four years; and to have this fruit in perfection plant out a portion every year. For this purpose we advise to plant those sorts that are called pistilate or female plants, allowing every sixth row to be of a variety that is called staminate or male plants. This latter sort keep within bounds, to prevent the runners intermingling with the bearing kinds. It is a prudent precaution to lay straw or other clean material between the rows of the fruiting plants, before they come into bloom, to prevent the fruit being injured by heavy rains, sand, or dust.

GATHERING THE FRUIT.—The common practice of picking the fruit with the footstalks attached, is one of the very worst systems, causing them to be handled and re-picked before they go to the table. Early in the morning take a vessel, basket, or box, of convenient size, and pick the fruit before it is softened by the sun. Lay hold of the calyx or cup at the base of the fruit, with the nail of the first finger and thumb of the left hand, and with the first finger of the right, give the fruit a gentle but quick draw, and it will come off into the hand without the least bruise or damage of any kind—and thus proceed till your vessel is full. Strawberries should go to the table without being turned or handled in any way, when the full, rich aroma of the fruit will be preserved. Those that are carried to market to be retailed for family use, should all be in portable boxes, in the same way as Raspberries. The present mode is disgusting in the extreme; large tubfuls, bruised and crushed, spooned into quart measures from vessels of very questionable character, in both color and appearance. The denizens carrying home their quantum of mashed matter, under the name of Strawberry, from such a mixture, can know little of the delicious aroma and rich flavor of the pure fruit called STRAWBERRY.

THE END.

www.ingramcontent.com/pod-product-compliance
Lightning Source LLC
LaVergne TN
LVHW011208110826
845150LV00006B/1363

* 9 7 8 1 4 2 5 5 1 8 5 6 1 *